PEER POWER, Book 2
STRATEGIES

for the Professional Leader

Applying Peer Helper Skills

Second Edition

Companion Book
For the Trainee—PEER POWER, Book 2
Applying Peer Helper Skills,
Second Edition (workbook)

Judith A. Tindall, Ph.D.
Psychologist, L.P.C., Consultant
Rohen and Associates
Psychological Center
St. Charles, Missouri

ACCELERATED DEVELOPMENT INC.
Publishers
Muncie, Indiana

Peer Power, Book 2,
Strategies for the Professional Leader:
Applying Peer Helper Skills, Second Edition

10 9 8 7 6 5 4 3 2 1

Printed in the United States of America

Technical Development: Virginia Cooper
Delores Kellogg
Cynthia Long
Marguerite Mader
Janet Merchant
Sheila Sheward

ISBN: 1-55959-060-2

Order additional copies from

ACCELERATED DEVELOPMENT INC.
PUBLISHERS
3808 West Kilgore Avenue
Muncie, Indiana 47304-4896
Toll Free Order Number 1-800-222-1166

DEDICATION

Peer Power, Book 2, Strategies for the Professional Leader: Applying Peer Helper Skills is dedicated to those professional leaders who have gone the extra mile and continued training peers to have an impact on others. The energy and time it takes to make truly successful programs comes from peer helpers becoming resources to others as opposed to just gaining new skills. This book is designed to provide you with guidelines you need as a trainer to teach others advanced application skills in groups, tutoring, health issues, leadership, and self-awareness. It was a decision to have this as a separate book because often trainers need their own training guide. If you need help in ideas for implementation of your program, please refer to *Peer Programs: An In-depth Look at Peer Helping.*

TABLE OF CONTENT

*Modules 1 through 13 are in *Peer Power, Book 1, Workbook: Becoming an Effective Peer Helper and Conflict Mediator* and in *Peer Power, Book 1, Strategies for the Professional Leader: Becoming an Effective Peer Helper and Conflict Mediator.*

INTRODUCTION

THE TRAINING PROGRAM

Peer Power, Book 2: Applying Peer Helper Skills is designed to assist your peer helpers to grow interpersonally, gain new skills, and have tools to work with others. They also will have an opportunity to develop a Code of Ethics and be involved in a Self-evaluation.

The manner in which you the professional decides how to utilize the following skills is up to you. The important aspect is that peer helpers have an opportunity to utilize their skills with others.

The eleven modules (14 through 24) may be taken in any order. Each is independent. The module on ethics (Module 24) is often the one that is used first.

Module 14 will help the peer helpers understand their own drug and alcohol use as well as recognize the problem in others. The will learn intervention skills.

Module 15, Stress Management—Moving toward Wellness, is designed first to assist the peer helper to assess his/her current ways of living and design a behavior change program to help create a healthier life-style. Then peer helpers can utilize the information to help others individually or in groups.

Module 16 is designed to assist peer helpers in learning techniques to enhance their self-esteem. In order for peer helpers to enhance others' self-esteem, peer helpers need to move toward being more fully functional themselves. Since peer helpers are models for others, they must focus on their strengths and strengths of others.

As peer helpers become more skilled in communicating with others, serving others individually and in groups, it is important for them to learn specific leadership skills, In doing Module 17, peer helpers will examine their current leadership styles and techniques to serve others.

One strategy that has been utilized throughout the time of man is the skill of tutoring others. Module 18 will guide the peer helper through steps to become an effective tutor.

If you decide to utilize peer helpers in a group setting, they will need specific skills. Module 19 will assist the peer helper in leading small groups that can be problem focused, growth focused, or task focused.

You may want peer helpers to teach lessons in the classroom of a school, business, or industrial setting; therefore, Module 20 will assist peer helpers in classroom presentation skills. Peer helpers can present exercises from various modules in this book such as wellness, eating disorders, drug and alcohol awareness, coping with loss, and suicide prevention.

At times, peer helpers need help in recognizing any eating problem they may have as well as how to recognize an eating disorder in others. Module 21 will assist peer helpers in learning about anorexia, bulimia, and compulsive overeating.

Peer helpers need to have skills in recognizing suicidal signals in others and know how to refer to professionals. Module 22 will assist in this skill.

Peer helpers can be effective in helping peers in systems through the grief process, which Module 23 can assist in doing.

Module 24 will help you lead the peer helpers through dealing with ethical issues and knowing how to refer. This may be the module with which to start. This module and others may be utilized in any order.

My hope is that you will utilize these exercised to meet your own curriculum design. You may use some or all of the exercises.

It is important that peer helpers have a foundation in the basic skills that can be found in *Peer Power, Book 1, Workbook: Becoming an Effective Peer Helper* and *Strategies for the Professional Leader, Third Edition.*

TIME LINES OF THE TRAINING MODULES

An approximation of the amount of time that needs to be allotted for each module has been included to facilitate scheduling requirements for the entire training program. Modifications can be made in the suggested time schedule to facilitate the maximum growth of trainees with whom one is working; however, with the first group of trainees, the recommendation is that one adheres fairly closely to the suggested time schedule. Figure 1 is an outline of the time schedule for Modules 14 through 24.

Book 2 (Applying Peer Helper Skills)

14	Drugs and Alcohol	430 - 505	205	12 - Adult
15	Wellness/Stress	400 - 480	260	12 - Adult
16	Enhancing Self Esteem	380 - 450	230	12 - Adult
17	Leadership Training	330 - 390	85	12 - Adult
18	Facilitating Small Group Discussion	330 - 520	105	12 - Adult
19	Leading Classroom Discussion	510 - 630	260	12 - Adult
20	Peer Helping Through Tutoring	330 - 580	360	12 - Adult
21	Recognizing Eating Disorders	330 - 480	205	12 - Adult
22	Suicide Prevention	180 - 270	150	12 - Adult
23	Coping With Loss	240 - 270	120	12 - Adult
24	Ethical Considerations	390 - 520		All
	TOTAL FOR BOOK 2			
	in minutes	3850 - 5095	1980	
	in hours	64-85	33	

NOTE: The time is further subdivided by Exercise, which can be taught individually or combined where needed.

Figure 1. Approximate time schedule for training session time and for homework time for each module.

The total time requirement will depend upon several factors such as ability and or prior experience of trainees, time block for each training session, and opportunity for practice and preparation between training sessions. Because training conditions will vary from location to location, the training program is organized into modules with subdivisions (exercises) that can be taught individually or combined to meet local conditions.

The overall approximate times by modules are provided in Figure 1. For planning the training program, times can be used for guides. When exercises are grouped for being taught in the same module, the total time span probably will be less than when each exercise is taught separately.

PHYSICAL ARRANGEMENT AND EQUIPMENT

The physical arrangements for a peer helping training program can be very simple or elaborate. The room must be large enough for role-playing to occur simultaneously in as many clusters as one-third the enrollment in each training session. Acoustics are important because of the interaction desired among trainees during the training sessions.

A chalkboard or flip pad or flannel board is helpful. Some means of writing notes large enough for viewing by all trainees is important.

Video and audio equipment for recording and playback are helpful for reinforcement and mobility. Trainees often are able to benefit from video viewing of previously prepared tapes of skills being taught and of tapes made of themselves during roleplaying.

Each trainee needs to have a copy of *Peer Power, Book 2 (workbook for trainee): Applying Peer Helper Skills* and the leader will need this copy of *Peer Power, Book 2, Strategies for the Professional Leader: Applying Peer Helper Skills.*

NUMBER AND AGE OF TRAINEES

The number of trainees in any given program is limited by the number of trainers, persons (potential trainees) available, facilities, and need for peer helpers once the training program is completed. A very minimum number at one time to facilitate the interaction suggested in many of the exercises is three. The maximum number with one peer helping professional probably would be 12, with six to nine being more ideal.

The age span generally is adolescent through adult.

FORMAT OF TRAINING SUGGESTIONS

Each module and exercise has purposes, introductory information, training procedures in sequential order, and homework assignment for trainees between training sessions. The trainer may want to audio tape or videotape some of the training to assist trainees.

MODULES
for
PEER POWER, BOOK 2
APPLYING PEER HELPER SKILLS
(WORKBOOK for TRAINEE)

MODULE **14**

DRUGS AND ALCOHOL ABUSE—INTERVENTION AND PREVENTION

Purposes

1. To enable trainees to learn some introductory material concerning the problem.

2. to become aware of their own chemical use, and

3. to look at alternative ways for coping with life.

Approximate Time

Module 14—Introduction Homework—10 to 15 minutes

Exercise 14.1—60 to 120 minutes in training session
Homework—60 to 120 minutes

Exercise 14.2—30 to 60 minutes in training session
Homework—20 minutes

Exercise 14.3—60 to 120 minutes in training session
Homework—60 minutes

Exercise 14.4—60 to 120 minutes in training session

Exercise 14.5—15 to 30 minutes in training session
Homework—60 minutes

Exercise 14.6-30 to 60 minutes
Homework—15 minutes

Exercise 14.7—60 to 120 minutes in training session

Exercise 14.8—60 to 120 minutes in training session
Homework—30 minutes

Exercise 14.9—60 minutes in training session
Homework—15 minutes

Materials

Peer Power, Book 2, Applying Peer Helper Skills (workbook), one copy for each trainee

Optional: Video equipment with video tape of the confrontation and intervention

Speaker on Alcohol and Substance Abuse

Film on the chemical problem

Book—Alcoholism: Causes, Effects, Treatment by Joseph Perez, Accelerated Development Inc., 3808 W. Kilgore Avenue, Muncie, IN 47304-4896.

Introduction to Module

Drug and alcohol abuse has been one of the major problems facing Americans today. In part, it is a problem because many individuals lack awareness of how chemicals affect their minds and bodies and thus, have a difficult time learning how to lead a healthy, happy life free of chemicals, suggest activities and relationships that can be helpful, and train peer counselors in the use of confrontation when intervention is necessary for a friend or family member.

Trainers may want to supplement this module with speakers and films concerning drugs and alcohol. They also may want to use the form in Exercise SD1.2, *Peer Power, Book 1, Becoming an Effective Peer Helper and Conflict Mediator,* for setting goals.

Training Procedures

1. Decide number of training sessions and exercises to be included in each.

2. Review content to be covered and suggested activities as listed in *Peer Power, Book 2, Applying Peer Helper Skills* (workbook).

3. Be prepared to do demonstration of confrontation as suggested or have videotapes of behaviors to be taught.

4. If a speaker or film is used, the trainer may want to schedule it in the early part of training. The National Council on Alcoholism has excellent films at reasonable cost.

Evaluation Process

As trainer, one can evaluate the process used in teaching a skill by the feedback obtained from trainees and by observations of their written work and their behavior when practicing the skill during training sessions.

Measuring Outcomes

1. Use Exercise 14.1 concerning the review quiz and puzzle and Exercise 14.2 and 14.3 to identify the effects of chemicals and the awareness of use.

2. Use Exercises 14.4 and 14.5 to examine the process and awareness of alternative approaches to drugs and alcohol.

3. Watch and listen closely during the role-playing in Exercise 14.7 to measure the ease with which trainees are using confrontation in terms of intervention.

EXERCISE 14.1
CHECKING MY KNOWLEDGE OF DRUGS AND ALCOHOL

Purpose

To learn some of the symptoms of alcoholism and drug abuse to become aware of the problems caused.

Introduction to Module

In Exercise 14.1, trainees will learn about the effects of alcohol and drug abuse. They will learn about how serious the chemical problem is, perhaps with someone they know. This exercise is designed to make them aware of these problems.

Training Procedures

1. Discuss with trainees the material presented concerning drugs and alcohol.

2. The trainer may want to show a film or ask a speaker to talk to the group concerning the effects of chemicals.

3. "Twenty-six Questions" is excellent to assess the trainees' personal use or friends' use of alcohol.

4. Ask trainees to complete the "Drug and Alcohol Review Quiz" and to review the "Common Signs of Other Drug Use."

5. The trainees will have a hard time believing the effects of drugs and alcohol and may even challenge the trainer concerning the problem. The purpose is not to get into a debate but to encourage them to do further reading about the problem.

6. Assign Exercise 14.1 sheets for homework.

Homework for Trainees after Group Meeting

1. Ask trainees to complete Exercise 14.1 by the next meeting.

2. Prepare for Exercise 14.2.

EXERCISE 14.2
STAGES OF ADOLESCENT CHEMICAL USE

Purposes

1. To provide trainees the opportunity to understand that chemical abuse happens in stages.

2. To help adolescents to examine their own use as well as that of others.

Introduction to Exercise

In Exercise 14.1, the trainees learned about the effect of chemicals. In Exercise 14.2, the trainees will learn about their own and others' chemical use and how it affects them.

Training Procedures

1. Review the material from Exercise 14.1.

2. Discuss the material in Exercise 14.2 in terms of whether or not the trainees agree with it.

3. Emphasize trust which is very important in proceeding with this exercise.

4. Ask the trainees to identify others whom they know and in what stage they are.

5. Ask the trainees to examine the different stages and decide in which stage they are. If any of the trainees bring up

their own problems, they may need to be referred to outside help.

6. Ask them what they learned from the activity.

7. Ask the trainees to turn in their homework from Exercise 14.1.

Homework

Ask trainees to prepare for Exercise 14.3.

EXERCISE 14.3
MY OWN CHEMICAL USE

Purpose

To provide trainees an opportunity to assess their own chemical use.

Introduction to Exercise

In Exercise 14.1, trainees learned about the effect of chemicals. In Exercise 14.2, they learned the stages of adolescent chemical use. In Exercise 14.3 trainees will learn about their own use of chemicals and how it affects them.

Training Procedures

1. Review the material from Exercise 14.1, 14.2, and from the speaker.

2. Discuss the material in terms of whether or not trainees agree with it.

3. Ask trainees to identify others they know who have had a chemical problem.

4. Ask trainees to turn in homework from Exercise 14.2.

5. Ask trainees to examine their own chemical use. Use the exercise as a guide for discussion.

6. Ask them what they learned from the activity.

7. This exercise will be helpful if the training group really trusts each other. They should be trusting by this time.

8. Some trainees may have a problem with chemicals. One might suggest they seek outside assistance.

9. Have the trainees set goals concerning chemical use of how they would like to change their life this week.

Homework for Trainees after Group Meeting

Ask trainees to work on their goal concerning chemicals for the week.

EXERCISE 14.4
TWENTY THINGS I LOVE TO DO AND MEANINGFUL RELATIONSHIPS

Purpose

To provide an opportunity for trainees to examine their activities and relationships and to see if they are leading to a healthy, fulfilling life.

Introduction to Exercise

As individuals begin to turn away from drugs and alcohol abuse and look to a healthier life-style, or as they begin to look at ways to prevent abuse, it is important to look at the kinds of activities they love to do and the type of relationships they have.

This exercise can be used in two ways: to see if the activities and relationships are helping trainees lead a chemical-free life, and to change the activities and relationships if they represent an unhealthy life-style. It is important first to examine these areas.

Training Procedures

1. Refer to the "Twenty Things I Love to Do." Encourage trainees to start filling out their lists by suggesting, "They can be big things or little things." One might offer an example or two or perhaps suggest, "You might think in terms of the seasons of the year for things you love to do." As trainer, draw up own list of twenty items. Explain to trainees that it is all right if they have more or less than twenty items on their lists.

2. When the lists are done, tell the students to use the rows of boxes on their papers to code their lists in the following manner.

    a. A dollar sign ($) is to be placed beside any item that costs more than $5 each time it is done.

    b. The letter A is to be placed beside those items the trainee really prefers to do alone.

       The letter P, next to activities that the trainee prefers to do with other persons.

       The letters A-P, next to activities that the trainee enjoys doing equally alone or with other persons.

    c. The letters PL are to be placed beside those that require planning.

d. The coding N5 is to be placed next to those items that would not have been listed five years ago.

e. The numbers 1 through 5 are to be placed beside the five most important items. The best loved activity should be number 1, the second best 2, and so on.

f. The trainee is to indicate next to each activity when (day, date) it was last engaged in.

g. Place a C beside any activity that includes chemicals.

h. Use the following additional suggestions for coding:

R—-Those things on the list that have an element of ***risk*** to them (physical, emotional or intellectual risk).

I—Any item that involves ***intimacy.***

S—Any item that can be done only in a particular ***season*** of the year.

Q—Any item that you think you would enjoy more if you were ***smarter.***

U—Any item that you think others would tend to judge as ***unconventional.***

C—Any item that you think others would tend to judge as ***conventional.***

MT—Any item that you think you will want to devote increasingly ***more time*** to in years to come.

CH—Any item that you hope your own ***children*** will have on their lists someday.

RE—Any item for which nobody would ***reject*** you just because you love to do it.

3. Discuss with the trainees their results.

   Do they see a pattern?

   Ask under what circumstance they like to engage in a chosen activity.

   Ask the trainees to look at the items listed in direction 1 think of advantages, pleasures, gains, benefits, or satisfactions they gain from the activity.

   Ask them if the activities are chemical-free or is this part of their lives?

4. If desired, give the trainees this activity after the end of training to see if this is different.

5. Have trainees look at Assessment of Meaningful Relationships and select 10 friends that are most significant to them today. Assess each friend selected according to the requirements of the worksheet.

6. Discuss results.

   Did they discover anything about themselves?

   Were they surprised?

   Were they disappointed in what they uncovered?

   How many of the relationships involve spending time with chemicals?

7. Ask trainees to think about their activities and relationships and to set any goals to make changes in either.

Homework for Trainees after Group Meeting

Ask trainees to work on goals for different activities and relationships.

EXERCISE 14.5
PERSONAL INVENTORY

Purposes

1. To help trainees to consider alternative highs from other activities.

2. To help trainees think of alternative highs for any group to which they belong.

Introduction to Exercise

1. Ask trainees how they are doing with their goals from Exercises 14.2, 14.3, and 14.4 and ask them to set future goals (30 minutes).

2. Ask trainees to list ways they get high other than from chemicals. There is a list suggested, but assist them in coming up with other ways. Ask them to explain these issues in a written form.

3. Ask students to circle any of the stereotypes they fit into, and ask if they would like to change.

4. Help students explore ways in which the group to which they belong can find an alternative high.

5. Help trainees set goals concerning alternative highs and changing stereotypes.

Homework for Trainees after Group Meeting

Ask trainees to continue working on goals for Exercise 14.4 and to begin working on goals for Exercise 14.5. Examples of alternative highs might be to learn to play tennis, go jogging, plan a dance for the school, ask a good friend to go to a movie, or prepare a gourmet meal.

EXERCISE 14.6
RECOGNIZING PROBLEMS IN OTHERS

Purpose

To help trainees to examine the behavior in others in terms of their chemical use and how this affects them and what they would like to have done. This is helpful when trying to do confrontation.

Introduction to Exercise

Peer counselors are often called on to help when someone wants to confront another person with their chemical use. The following exercise will help the trainee keep a journal.

Training Procedures

1. Discuss the reaction to Exercise 14.5.

2. Have the trainees write things that have happened when a family member or friend abused chemicals.

3. Have the trainees write the date and behavior:

   My feelings, my reaction, what I would like to see done. For example:

   > 6/25 Drank so much passed out at party/Angry, frustrated/Cried/ You're not to drink at parties.

4. From the chart, have them make a plan of confrontation.

Guidelines for Confrontation

1. Confrontation is an individualized plan of action.

2. Confrontation must be done out of love, not malice, resentment, or retaliation.

a. Must be made when the chemical abuser is not under the influence and at an appropriate time and place.

b. A genuine statement must be sent: "I feel ______________."

c. Circumstances must be stated simply.

d. Must be calm and caring.

3. Before confrontation is made, you must develop:

A sense of direction.
A sense of confidence.
A sense of well-being.

Homework for Trainees after Group Meeting

Continue with the chart and plan.

EXERCISE 14.7
PUTTING CONFRONTATION INTO ACTION

Purpose

To help trainees use their skills in confrontation, assertiveness, and genuineness in an intervention activity.

Introduction to Exercise

Peer counselors are often put in the position of being aware that someone is having a chemical problem. It is frustrating not knowing what to do about the problem. Sometimes it is good to work with a professional counselor to help facilitate the confrontation concerning drugs and alcohol. This activity also can be used with a friend or family member.

Training Procedures

1. Discuss intervention and the purpose of intervention. Suggest the option of having a professional counselor present.
2. Ask trainees to divide into groups of three.
3. Ask the group members to choose one of the situations given or one with which they are familiar.
4. Have each trainee play one of three roles: the confronter, the person with the problem, and the facilitator.
5. Rotate around the groups to discuss the activity.
6. As trainer, role-play one of the situations.
7. Encourage trainees to use all the skills they have learned thus far.
8. Discuss the experience.

Homework for Trainees after Group Meeting

Continue to work on your own personal goals and read introduction to Exercise 15.1.

EXERCISE 14.8
FAMILIES AFFECTED BY ALCOHOLISM

Purpose

To focus on the effect of alcohol on the family.

Introduction to Exercise

Alcoholism not only affects the alcoholic but it also affects their family. An important aspect of this exercise is to assist trainees in identifying symptoms and finding some help for the dysfunctional family.

Training Procedures

1. Discuss the intervention and the purpose of the intervention from Exercise 14.7.
2. If possible to obtain, show a film or video on adult children of alcoholics or on addiction is a family affair.
3. Ask the trainees to read the material from this exercise and discuss each point.
4. Ask the trainees if they identify with some of the roles in the family of an alcoholic.
5. Focus on the differences in the body reaction of a social drinker versus that of an alcoholic drinker.
6. Help the trainees focus on their own family in terms of possible alcoholism.
7. Help the trainees to focus on others by having them role-play with one person being the child of an alcoholic and another playing the helper and using the information available.
8. Refer them to the appropriate outside help.
9. Have the peer counselors write for information.

Homework for Trainees after Group Meeting

Have the trainees write their reaction to the activity.

EXERCISE 14.9
JUST SAY "NO"

Purpose

To help the trainees practice saying "No" to peer pressure.

Introduction to Exercise

Peer counselors are role models for others in terms of leading a healthy life-style. This exercise is to be used by the training group; at other times it could be used in groups that the peer counselor facilitates or in a classroom presentation.

The trainees need to be encouraged to identify levels of alcohol use in themselves and others and to identify peer pressures to use alcohol in social, party settings. The trainees need to realize that the danger of alcohol lies in the relative ease in obtaining it and its social acceptability over other drugs. The trainees need to see the positive consequences of nonuse or use in moderation (as an adult), and the negative consequences of misuse, abuse, and dependence. The trainees should be asked to define the difference between use and abuse of alcohol and to express ways of avoiding peer pressure to misuse alcohol.

Terms: Nonuse=Avoidance of alcohol
Use=Use of alcohol in moderation

Training Procedures

1. Discuss peer pressure and its meaning.

2. Discuss the terms nonuse, use, abuse, and dependence. Ask for examples of each.

3. Discuss the concept of peer pressure. Ask for definitions and/or examples. Peer pressure has no age limit. Give them examples of peer pressure in the young and old as well as outcomes such as vandalizing or buying a certain car.

4. Discuss how easily students are exposed to alcohol by asking them about their personal introduction to it. Be sure to bring out the party setting. Talk about parties and what these mean.

5. Discuss how some individuals misuse alcohol at parties. give examples.

6. Ask the members to discuss the consequences of nonuse and abuse.

7. Ask the trainees how they can put a limit on their use.

8. Divide the group into triads. Ask them to role-play a party where all are drinking. One person decides to say "No." Change roles so that all of the members have a chance to play each role.

9. Lead a discussion on consequences.

Homework for Trainees after Group Meeting

Write how it felt to say, "No."

MODULE **15**

STRESS MANAGEMENT— MOVING TOWARD WELLNESS

Purpose

To help trainees become aware of their own stressors and to learn effective techniques for coping with stress and moving toward a life-style of wellness.

Approximate Time

Module 15—Introduction Homework—60 minutes

Exercise 15.1—60 minutes in training session
Homework—60 minutes

Exercise 15.2—60 minutes in training session
Homework—60 minutes

Exercise 15.3—60 minutes in training session
Homework—60 minutes

Exercise 15.4—60 minutes in training session
Homework—30 minutes

Exercise 15.5—30 minutes in training session
Homework 30 minutes

Exercise 15.6—30 minutes in training session
Homework—30 minutes

Exercise 15.7—60 minutes in training session
Homework—30 minutes

Exercise 15.8—60 minutes in training session
Homework—20 minutes

Exercise 15.9—60 minutes in training session
Homework—60 minutes

Exercise 15.10—60 minutes in training session

Materials

Peer Power, Book 2, Applying Peer Helper Skills (workbook), one copy for each trainee

Chalkboard and chalk or flip pad and pen

Optional: Film on wellness or stress

Introduction to Module

In this module, trainees will have an opportunity to learn about stress and wellness. The trainer may want to use the goal setting materials described in Exercise SD1.2, *Peer Power, Book 1, Becoming an Effective Peer Helper and Conflict Mediator,* to assist in changes in behavior. It is important for the leaders to model kinds of responses that they want the trainees to use. This module is a skill that naturally follows the drug and alcohol module, because it assists trainees in moving toward a healthier life-style. This module is simply an introduction to stress management and wellness. For changes to be permanent, we would suggest working with a group for a minimum of 12 meetings on changing life-styles (this could be in weight loss, stopping smoking, exercise). The important thing is to help trainees become aware of how they need to make some changes.

Training Procedures

1. Decide on groups of exercises for the training sessions. The decision will make a difference in homework assignments and the time available for each exercise.

2. Follow the sequence of exercises and the training procedures for each.

3. Arrange for films, if used.

4. Arrange for goal setting sheets to be available to trainees.

5. Model each exercise with trainer expressing their stressors and so forth.

Evaluation Process

As a trainer, evaluate the process used in the teaching of the skill by the feedback obtained from trainees and by observations of written work and of their behavior when they are asked to set some goals.

Measuring Outcomes

1. Use Exercises 15.1, 15.2, and 15.3 to identify stressors, stress reaction, and effective techniques for coping with stressors.

2. Use Exercise 15.5 to look at setting goals for a balanced life-style. Use Exercise 15.9 for setting long-range goals.

EXERCISE 15.1
WHAT HAPPENS UNDER STRESS?

Purpose

To enable trainees to understand stress and to help them identify events that cause stress in their lives.

Introduction to Exercise

This exercise is designed to help trainees learn about stress and to discuss the issue of stress with their trainer. The trainer may decide to show a film on stress and wellness. The exercise is most beneficial to trainees; it helps them to identify stressors through the personal appraisal form.

Training Procedures

1. Review goals set from Module 14 and assess progress.

2. Review the introductory material to this module and that for Exercise 15.1.

3. Show a film on stress and wellness if available.

4. Discuss the whole area of stress and wellness and, for those who are interested, suggest some of the related books listed in the trainer's manual.

5. Ask trainees to fill out the personal appraisal form to help identify stressors.

6. Discuss the responses.

   Example:

   > When are you feeling most stressed? Around whom do you feel most stressed? What did you learn about yourself concerning your stressors?

Homework for trainees after Group Meeting

1. Continue working on goals from Module 14 and setting new goals.

2. Recognize stressors in your life during the next week (day).

3. Read Exercise 15.2 on effects of stress.

EXERCISE 15.2
EFFECTS OF STRESS ON ME

Purpose

To enable trainees to understand the effects of stress on the individual both in a positive and negative manner.

Introduction to Exercise

This exercise is designed to help trainees learn about stress and its positive and negative effects. The idea is to convey that stress can be both positive and negative and to assist the trainees in identifying how stress affects them.

Training Procedures

1. Review goals from Module 14 and assess progress.
2. Review stressors and discuss their discovery of additional stressors.
3. Ask trainees to review positive and negative effects of stress.
4. Have trainees work with a partner to help identify effects of stress on them.
5. Discuss results.
6. Have trainees turn in Exercise 15.2 for trainer feedback.

Homework for Trainees after Group Meeting

1. Continue to work on goals from Module 14.
2. Begin to identify positive and negative effects of stress on trainee.

EXERCISE 15.3
COPING WITH STRESSORS

Purpose

To assist trainees in examining effective and ineffective techniques for coping with stressors.

Introduction to Exercise

Review Exercises 15.1 and 15.2 and return material handed in. This is a very important exercise and begins to help trainees learn new ways of coping with stress.

Training Procedures

1. List stressors and how they affect the trainee (reaction). The trainer models what he/she want by using the chalkboard.
2. Have trainees discuss stressors and their effects.
3. Ask trainees to work with a partner to develop how they can handle stress (both ineffectively and effectively).
4. The trainer then asks the group to list effective and ineffective techniques for coping with stress. List methods on a chalkboard and have someone else record them on paper in a form for duplicating for the group. This may assist group members in coming up with effective techniques.
5. Refer to goal setting techniques from Exercise SD1.2, *Peer Power, Book 1, Becoming an Effective Peer Helper and Conflict Mediator.*
6. Ask trainees to try a new effective coping technique.

Homework for Trainees after Group Meeting

Work on a goal to change by handling stressor differently.

EXERCISE 15.4
UNDERSTANDING THE DIFFERENCE BETWEEN TENSION AND RELAXATION THROUGH IMAGERY

Purpose

To enable the trainees to know the difference between tension and relaxation.

Introduction to Exercise

This exercise uses imagery to help the trainees visualize tension and relaxation. Please have the room as quiet as possible and the light low. You may want to use some quiet music in the background.

Training Procedures

1. Read the following script in a calm, even voice:

   Please get as comfortable as possible and close your eyes to better feel the contrast between tension and relaxation. If you are worried about other things, please put those aside for a while. Today we are going to practice paying attention to how we feel. Sometimes our bodies let us know how we feel before our minds do. Please do not talk. I will be asking you questions, but think about the answers and keep your answers to yourself.

   We are now ready to begin. Please follow my directions exactly and concentrate on what you are feeling. First, close your eyes. Keeping your eyes closed, sit in your chair so that you feel comfortable. Think to yourself, how am I sitting? Are my legs stretched out or are they crossed? Are my arms at my side or folded? Am I sitting up straight or slouching? Think about how you are sitting and how you feel right Now. (PAUSE HERE FOR A FEW SECONDS.) *Keeping your eyes closed, next make a frown with your face. Frown as much as you can. Frown harder. . . . harder. Keep frowning and as you frown, think about how your face feels. Think about, does it hurt? How do your eyebrows feel? How do your cheeks feel? How does your mouth feel? Okay, stop frowning. Keeping your eyes closed, think about how your face feels now. Does it feel differently than when you were frowning? How do your eyebrows feel? Keeping your eyes closed, think about how your face feels now. Does it feel differently than when you were frowning? How do your eyebrows feel? How do your cheeks feel? How does your mouth feel?*

Now, keeping your eyes closed, ball both hands into a fist. Ball the fists as tightly as you can and place your arms down at your sides, keeping your fists balled tightly. Think about how you feel right now. How do your fingers feel? How do your arms feel? How do your shoulders feel? (PAUSE FOR A FEW SECONDS.) *Now unball your fists and relax. Keeping your eyes closed, think about how you feel right now. How do your fingers feel? How do your arms feel? How do your shoulders feel? Do you feel differently now than you did when you had your fists balled tightly? Think about how you felt with your fists balled and how you feel now.* (PAUSE FOR A FEW SECONDS.)

Now, keeping your eyes closed, inhale and, as you inhale, try to hold in your stomach until it touches your back. Think about how you feel right now. How does your chest feel? How does your stomach feel? Exhale and relax. Think about how you feel right now. How does your chest feel? How does your stomach feel? Do you feel differently now than you did when you were holding your breath? (PAUSE FOR A FEW SECONDS.)

Now, keeping your eyes closed, stretch your legs out in front of you. Curl your toes under as tightly as you can. Think about how you feel right now. How do your toes feel? How do your legs feel? Do they hurt? Now uncurl your toes, unstretch your legs, and relax. Keeping your eyes closed, think about how you feel right now. How do your toes feel? How do your legs feel? Do they hurt? Think about how you felt with your toes curled under and your legs stretched and how you feel now. (PAUSE FOR A FEW SECONDS.)

Now, keeping your eyes closed, make a frown with your face, ball your fists as tightly as you can, and place your arms down at your sides; hold in your breath and hold in your stomach until it touches your back. Stretch your legs out in front of you and curl your toes. Keeping eyes closed, think about how you feel right now. Okay, exhale, but keep the frown on your face, your fists balled, your legs stretched, and your toes curled. Think about how you feel right now. Okay, stop frowning, but keep your fists balled, your legs stretched, and your toes curled. Think about how you feel right now. Okay, unball your fists, but keep your legs stretched and your toes curled. Think about how you feel right now. Okay, now relax your legs and toes. Think about how you feel right now. Keep your eyes closed. Think about how your face feels. Think about how your shoulders feel. Think about how your arms feel. Think about how your shoulders feel. Think about how your arms feel. Think about how your fingers feel. Think about how your chest feels. Think about how your stomach feels. Think about how your legs feel. Think about how your toes feel. Keep your eyes closed and relax. Now open your eyes.

2. Have the trainees draw a picture of both relaxation and tension. You may even want them to color the pictures.

3. Ask the trainees to answer questions about the images.

4. Lead a discussion with questions from the trainees' worksheets.

5. Have pictures shared by those who are willing.

6. Try to get the idea of using images to feel relaxed.

7. Lead a discussion on how both relaxation and tension relieve stress.

Homework for trainees after Group Meeting

1. Ask the trainees to think about their image of relaxation and imagine this at least twice a day.

2. Read and prepare for Exercise 15.5.

EXERCISE 15.5
BALANCED HEALTHY LIFE

Purpose

To provide an opportunity for trainees to look at how balanced their lives are and to examine how they may want to change their lives.

Introduction to Exercise

Ask the trainees to think about their life and about a balance toward a healthier life-style. The trainer will have to use several examples for trainees to understand the concept of "out of balance." Only if we help manage stress at all levels of their lives are we able to move toward wellness.

Training Procedures

1. Review goals from Exercise 15.4 and answer any questions.

2. Explain that today the training will involve looking at the "total you" to see if anything is out of balance.

3. Optional: Ask one trainee to stand in the middle of a circle. Have another representing "diet" move clockwise around the circle. Ask another trainee to move counterclockwise representing "emotional." Proceed until everyone is moving in either a clockwise or counterclockwise direction and then ask the "physical" to sit down. Ask

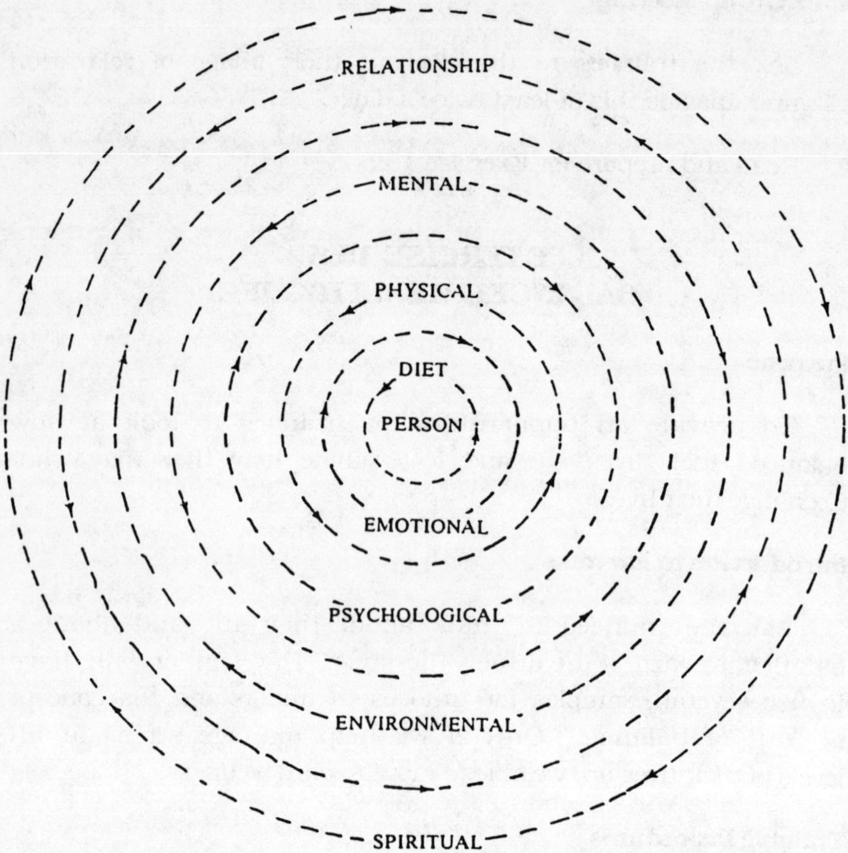

the others to stop and discuss with them the interaction of all areas and what happens when one part stops.

4. Ask them to think about their own lives.

Are they eating balanced meals?
Are they feeling good most of the time?
Are they getting adequate exercise (vigorous exercise three times a week)?
Are they feeling okay psychologically?
Are they able to think and concentrate and problem solve?

Are they living in a healthy environment?
Do they have supportive friends and family?
Do they have a spiritual outlet? Additional questions.

5. Ask trainees to set goals to deal with an area that is out of balance. They should not work on more than one area at a time.

   Example: "I will exercise three times a week by running two miles each time."

Homework for Trainees after Group Meeting

1. Ask them to work on goal.
2. Read and complete Exercise 15.6.

EXERCISE 15.6 HEALTH HABITS AS A MEANS OF REDUCING STRESS

Purpose

To help the trainees get in touch with their life-styles and examine ways to change their life-styles.

Introduction to Exercise

The way we choose to live our lives has a lot to do with how long we live and how we handle stress and tension. In the trainee book is a checklist to help trainees get in touch with some simple ways to change their lives.

Training Procedures

1. Review the homework from the previous exercise.
2. Show a film or filmstrip that looks at these issues of wellness and healthy life-styles.

3. Lead a discussion on the above health habits.

4. Lead a discussion on how to help the trainees change their lives.

Homework for Trainees after Group Meeting

1. Develop a plan of action in terms of life change.

2. Read and complete Exercise 15.7.

EXERCISE 15.7
THOUGHTS, FEELINGS, BEHAVIOR

Purpose

1. To assist the trainees in understanding the differences among thoughts, feelings, and behavior.

2. To help the trainees understand how thoughts affect feelings and behavior.

Introduction to Exercise

When trainees and/or others are involved in a tense situation, trainees need to understand that they have a choice in terms of how they behave. Their behavior is influenced by thoughts and feelings. Vital for them is to understand that they can change their thoughts and hence their behavior.

Training Procedures

1. Review the homework from the last exercise.

2. Review the differences among thoughts, feelings, and behavior.

A = Thoughts
B = Feelings
C = Behavior

A + B = C

3. Demonstrate with role-playing situations two alternative ways of thinking and feeling and behavior.

4. Divide the group into triads and continue the role-playing situations along with other situations that they may want to introduce themselves and then ask them to write their thoughts, feelings, and behavior as well as alternative thoughts, feelings, and behavior.

5. While observing the role-playing activities, identify the trainees who have particular strengths in making up dialogues that illustrate accurately the situations. Give assistance to them. Additional practice sessions could be established with the trainees' own examples.

6. Lead a discussion centered around

   a. Do you see that the way we think about a situation often determines how we act?

   b. Do you understand that we all choose to behave in a certain way?

7. Have the trainees identify strong feelings in their personal life and come up with feelings and behavior.

Homework for Trainees after Group Meeting

1. Ask the trainees to identify strong feelings and thoughts and write them: have them consider alternative thoughts and feelings.

2. Read and complete Exercise 15.8.

EXERCISE 15.8
EXAMINING YOUR SUPPORT SYSTEM

Purpose

To enable the trainees to understand the need for a good support system.

Introduction to Exercise

This exercise is designed to help trainees learn about support systems and the help it can give them, how to expand their own support system and make opportunities to give their support system a change, and how they can support others.

Training Procedures

1. Review the homework from the previous exercise.
2. Discuss the fact that we all have "people needs" and that no one is self-sufficient, although some need people more than others.
3. Ask the trainees to make their lists of individuals with whom they have contact and what need they meet.
4. Ask the trainees to call out the needs that they have listed from their right-hand column on the chart, "Your Needs and Your Support System," as you put them on the board.
5. Review the lists and show that they generally fall into the following categories:

   Physical Needs: sex, food, shelter
   Psychological Needs: caring, understanding, listening, intimacy
   Social Needs: belonging status, group identity, helping others

6. Lead the trainees through a discussion concerning how often they see those individuals whom they feel they need, who makes contact, and is there a pattern?

7. Explore the next section in terms of improving the effectiveness of individual support systems by planning a support system so that one's needs do not go unmet.

8. Discuss the three columns in the chart in their workbooks; listed on the left-column of the chart is the type of support that individuals need; in the second column is one for work and school, and the third column is personal life. Each of the three columns is divided into "Present" and "Possible" columns.

9. Ask the trainees to brainstorm possible individuals who might supply support.

10. Focus on others whom we try to support and what function we play in terms of meeting others' needs.

Homework for Trainees after Group Meeting

1. Ask the trainees to write a paragraph concerning how to expand their own support system as well as how they can be supportive of others.

2. Read Exercise 15.9.

EXERCISE 15.9
HOW TO BEAT STRESS

Purpose

To provide a long-range plan to handle stress in a healthy manner.

Introduction to Exercise

How we choose to handle stress is an important factor of our well-being. Work with trainees to help them handle stress more effectively. It may be desired to take them through a relaxation exercise.

Training Procedures

1. Review goals from Exercise 15.8 and previous modules.

2. Ask trainees to review the list of how to beat stress.

3. Ask trainees to go through a relaxation activity. Have them sit comfortably with their eyes closed as trainer very slowly reads the following exercise. Ask them to quietly repeat each statement when finished.

   Relaxation Phrases

   a. I feel quite quiet.

   b. I am beginning to feel quite relaxed.

   c. The muscles in my toes and feet feel heavy and relaxed.

   d. The muscles in my calves, knees, thighs, and hips feel heavy and relaxed.

   e. My abdomen, solar plexus, and the whole central portion of my body feel heavy, relaxed, and comfortable.

   f. My fingers, hands, arms, and shoulders feel heavy, relaxed, and comfortable.

   g. My neck, jaws, eyes, and forehead feel relaxed. They feel comfortable and smooth.

   h. The muscles in my whole body feel heavy, comfortable, relaxed, and quiet.

i. Continue silently on your own, feeling this heaviness throughout the body and continuing the relaxation (take 1-2 minutes).

j. I am quiet relaxed.

k. My arms (legs) and hands (feet) feel heavy and warm.

l. I feel quite quiet.

m. My whole body is relaxed and my hands (feet) feel warm, relaxed and warm.

n. I can feel the warmth flowing down my arms (legs) into my hands (feet).

o. My hands are warm, toasty warm.

p. Warmth is flowing into my hands (feet); they are warm, very warm.

q. My hands (feet) are warm, relaxed and warm.

r. Continue silently on your own, feeling this warmth in the hands (feet) and fingers (toes) (take 1-2 minutes).

s. My whole body feels relaxed and my mind is quiet.

t. I have withdrawn my attention from the outside world, and I feel serene and still.

u. My attention is turned inward, and I feel at ease.

v. Within my mind I can visualize, imagine, and experience myself as relaxed, comfortable, and still.

w. I am aware in an easy, quiet, inward-turned way.

x. My mind is calm and quiet.

y. I feel an inward quietness.

z. I am at peace; I am at peace.

Continue silently on your own, feeling your own body as relaxed and feeling your mind as calm, quiet, and peaceful (take 1-2 minutes).

The relaxation is now concluded and the whole body is reactivated with a deep breath and the following phrases: (a) I feel life and energy flowing through my toes, feet, calves, knees, thighs, hips, solar plexus, chest, shoulders, arms, hands, fingers, neck, jaws, eyes, and head; (b) this energy makes me feel light and alive; (c) I open my eyes and make contact with the outside world; (d) I feel refreshed and good. (Stretch if desired).

4. Ask the trainees how they felt.

5. Ask them to identify a long-range goal. Have them fill out the long-range goal forms. Have the whole group listen to the goals and as trainer make comments.

Homework for Trainees after Group Meeting

1. Begin to implement a long-range goal.

2. Read and complete Exercise 15.10/

EXERCISE 15.10
LONG-RANGE GOALS

Purpose

To help the trainees set up long-range goals in terms of changing their life-style.

Introduction to Exercise

Help trainees know the importance of developing their goals. Tell them that as a group assistance will be given to set up specific activities for them to do to accomplish development of long-range goals.

Training Procedures

1. Review the homework from the previous exercise.

2. Ask the trainees to address long-range goals for themselves in terms of mental, physical, and emotional aspects.

3. Use the last sheet in their workbooks for this module to expand on their goal(s).

4. Divide the group into twos and review their long-range goal(s).

5. Ask the trainees to have you review those goals.

6. Discuss how a support system could assist them in reaching these goals.

Homework for Trainees after Group Meeting

1. Read the introduction to the next module.

2. Read and complete Exercise 16.1.

MODULE **16**

ENHANCING SELF-ESTEEM

Purpose

To help trainees assess their self-esteem and focus on their strengths.

Approximate Time

Module 16—Introduction Homework—10 to 15 minutes

Exercise 16.1—60 minutes in training session
Homework—30 minutes

Exercise 16.2—60 minutes in training session
Homework—20 minutes

Exercise 16.3—30 to 60 minutes in training session
Homework—30 minutes

Exercise 16.4—30 to 60 minutes in training session
Homework—30 minutes

Exercise 16.5—60 minutes in training session
Homework—30 minutes

Exercise 16.6—60 minutes in training session

Exercise 16.7—60 minutes in training session
Homework—30 minutes

Exercise 16.8—60 minutes in training session
Homework—30 minutes

Materials

Peer Power, Book 2, Applying Peer Helper Skills (workbook), one copy for each trainee

3 x 5 Cards

Introduction to Module

Trainer can use enhancing self-esteem exercises to help trainees develop positive feelings about themselves; to help them view themselves as capable of developing and changing through examination of their strengths, successes, and values; and to teach the trainee how to set and act on goals. A helpful resource is the book entitled *Enhancing Self Esteem, Second Edition* by D. Frey and C. J. Carlock (1989), published by Accelerated Development Inc., Muncie, IN.

It is important for the trainer to be structured, positive, and open, and to encourage and build these important feelings in trainees.

Training Procedures

1. Decide the number of training sessions and the exercises to be included in each.

2. Review the content to be covered and the suggested activities as listed in *Peer Power, Book 2, Applying Peer Helper Skills* (workbook).

3. Be prepared to be open and positive.

Evaluation Process

As trainer, evaluate the process used in teaching this skill by the feedback you are obtaining from the trainees and by observations of them in the group.

Measuring Outcomes

1. Use Exercise 16.1 to determine whether or not trainees can relate present self-confidence to past events.

2. Use Exercise 16.2 to determine whether or not trainees can understand the effects of both positive and negative messages.

3. use Exercise 16.3 to get acquainted with and tune into positive thinking.

4. Use Exercise 16.4 and 16.5 to help examine and clarify trainees' values.

5. Use Exercise 16.6 to see if trainees can acknowledge their strengths.

6. Use Exercise 16.7 to set short-term and long-term goals.

7. Use Exercise 16.8 to get feedback from others.

EXERCISE 16.1
CHECKLIST FOR SELF-ESTEEM

Purpose

To assist trainees in identifying their level of self-esteem and ways of enhancing their self-esteem.

Introduction to Exercise

The purpose of this exercise is to assess how trainees see themselves in terms of self-esteem. The checklist in this exercise might be good to give again at the end of the module to see whether or not the level of self-esteem has changed for the trainees. The last part of this module is designed to get the trainees to look at areas on which they need to work. You may want to refer them to other modules if they need additional help such as assertiveness training for speaking up.

Training Procedures

1. Review the introduction to see whether or not the trainees agree and have other things to add.
2. Ask the trainees to test themselves on the checklist.
3. Ask the trainees how they would rate themselves in terms of self-esteem. If they answer "Yes" to most of the items, then they need a lot of help. If they answer "Yes" to some items only, then these are the areas on which you can help them work.
4. Discuss ways to enhance self-esteem.
5. Help the trainees to develop individually a plan of action.

Homework for Trainees after Group Meeting

1. Ask them to observe themselves and how they react to others.
2. Read and complete Exercise 16.2.

EXERCISE 16.2
MESSAGES FROM THE PAST

Purpose

To get in touch with positive and negative messages from the past.

Introduction to Exercise

This is a powerful exercise. As a result of doing it, you may need to do a great deal of discussing and possibly make referrals for some participants.

Training Procedures

1. Review the homework from the last exercise.

2. Discuss the idea that our past influences the present, for example, what individuals whom we have known have said to us. Help the trainees to identify messages from the past that influence them today. "If it is worth doing, it is worth doing right." "You are a bum." "You are dumb." "You are fat."

3. Lead a discussion on how these messages still influence us today.

4. Discuss ways to change some of the messages.

Homework for Trainees after Group Meeting

1. Be aware of messages from the past.

2. Read and complete Exercise 16.3.

EXERCISE 16.3
STRENGTHS

Purpose

To assist trainees in identifying significant good events in their lives to help identify strengths, and to build cohesiveness.

Introduction to Exercise

The purpose of this exercise is to help trainees discover or rediscover their strengths, capabilities, and attributes—their own human potential.

"Although you will not be encouraged to take risks in this group, your experience will be most meaningful and productive if you behave as authentically as possible. So try constantly to be honest with the group and with yourself. The training group will be a very helpful resource for each of you."

"If you have authentically, you might reveal some things about yourself that you don't usually reveal. Therefore, the information that is shared in this module is confidential; it belongs only to this group. Do you agree?" (Clear up any doubts and/or questions about this before proceeding.)

Training Procedures

1. Review goals set from Module 15, the long-range planning, and the trainees' progress.

2. Read or summarize information from the introduction of the module.

3. Each group member will have five minutes to share with the others those significant events of his/her life.

   What were the good moments? The good events? The good relationships? What were your successes? Positive achievements? Rewards? Honors? Or simply good, meaningful, rewarding experiences?

   Just name them without complete sentences to give as many significant ones as possible within the time limit. Each of you will have five minutes.

4. Complete the written exercise for Exercise 16.3.

5. This is usually a very powerful experience.

Homework for Trainees after Group Meeting

1. Continue working on goals.

2. Continue thinking about positive experiences.

EXERCISE 16.4
PERSONAL COAT OF ARMS

NOTE: Our thanks to Sister Louis, Principal of St. Julian's School in Chicago in 1972.

Purpose

To help trainees publicly affirm things that they believe in and share these with the group.

Introduction to Exercise

The trainer could go into the significance of a coat of arms shield. The idea is to publicly affirm these values and things that are important and to share them with the group.

Training Procedures

1. Review goals from previous meetings.

2. Divide the coat of arms shield into six sections (see figure in *Peer Power, Book 2, Applying Peer Helper Skills* [workbook]). The trainer makes it clear that words are to be used only in the sixth block, all the others are to contain pictures. Stress that it is not an art lesson; only crude stick figures need be used. Review what goes into each section.

3. Ask trainees to share their coat of arms with the group. Encourage questions and comments.

4. Suggest that trainees take the coat of arms home and if they feel comfortable doing so, share it with their families.

5. Discuss experience. "I learned. . . . . . . "

   "I was surprised at . . . ."

Homework for Trainees after Group Meeting

Continue to work on goals from previous modules.

EXERCISE 16.5
VALUES AUCTION

NOTE: Recognition for the Values Auction is given to W. Clement Stone Foundation, *Achievement Motivation Program,* 111 E. Wacker Dr., Suite 510, Chicago, IL 60601.

Purpose

To publicly affirm values to other group members.

Introduction to Exercise

The values auction can be fun for the participants while helping them clarify their values.

Training Procedures

1. Check on past goals.
2. Read the directions in *Peer Power, Book 2, Applying Peer Helper Skills* (workbook), and assist the trainees in going through the activity.
3. Each item is discussed in terms of the value it represents. If their highest bid was $1,000, they would be able to assess this as their most important value.
4. The trainer plays the auctioneer.
5. This is generally an activity that the trainees enjoy.

Homework for Trainees after Group Meeting

Continue working on goals.

EXERCISE 16.6
STRENGTH ACKNOWLEDGEMENT

Purpose

This exercise is designed to assist the trainees in expressing their strengths.

Training Procedures

1. Review the goals on which the trainees are working.

2. Discuss the fact that focusing on strengths is difficult. The trainer should model the kind of discussion the group wants.

3. Ask for a volunteer to share a self-perceived strength.

4. Ask for comments from others.

5. A desirable procedure is to ask trainees if there is anything keeping them from using their strengths.

Homework for Trainees after Group Meeting

Continue working on goals.

EXERCISE 16.7 JOURNEY INTO LIFE: GOAL SETTING

Purpose

To assist trainees in short-term and long-term goal setting using some of their strengths.

Introduction to Exercise

This exercise is designed to help group members set short-term and long-term goals about something they will do.

Training Procedures

1. Review goals on which trainees are working.

2. Pass out note cards and ask participants to write short-term goals and share them with the group.

3. Ego reinforcement: When all have established their short-term goals say, "Now, look at your goal. Commit the entire statement to memory."

4. Have the group stand up and form a circle with arms around each other.

5. While they are together say, "Remember that we all have our recorders, our 'alter egos.' These are the only ones who have data about us because they record for us. So, during the week, let's each make copies of the personal data our recorders gave us and try to use it."

6. Ask them to write on the cards the following sentence stems and then complete each.

   a. If I had three wishes, they would be

   b. Two of my recent significant achievements are

   c. List one recent, significant failure or unresolved task or problem

   d. If I were to die, I would want to be remembered for

7. Divide into pairs. With your alter ego, set achievement goals for one year or longer. Talk about them.

8. Ask the trainees to write goals and give them to their partner to check on in one year.

Homework for Trainees after Group Meeting

Continue working on goals from previous modules.

EXERCISE 16.8 CONCLUSION

Purpose

To gain feedback concerning strengths from others in the group.

Introduction to Exercise

This is a powerful exercise and the trainees should feel very good about the experience. Tell the group to be serious.

Training Procedures

1. Check on previous goals.

2. Distribute cards so that each trainee has a separate card for every other group member.

3. Have each participant write a positive statement about every other trainee. These statements must be strengths or attributes, only good qualities. Tell the group to mean what they say and to be spontaneous. Then have them add an "I urge you to ______________________________" on the back of each card. This focuses on suggested change.

4. Discuss the cards

5. Give participants the cards written about themselves.

6. This activity may take one or two training sessions.

Homework for Trainees after Group Session

1. Work on short-term and long-term goals.

2. Review the cards given to you.

3. Read the introduction to Module 17.

MODULE **17**

LEADERSHIP TRAINING

Purpose

To enable trainees to examine their leadership style and to develop techniques for leading a group, such as action plans, and planning a meeting.

Approximate Time

Module 17-Introduction
Homework—10 to 15 minutes of homework

Exercise 17.1—60 minutes in training session

Exercise 17.2—60 to 90 minutes in training session
Homework—30 minutes

Exercise 17.3—60 to 90 minutes in training session
Homework—30 minutes

Exercise 17.4—60 minutes in training session
Homework—60 minutes

Exercise 17.5—30 minutes in training session

Exercise 17.6—60 minutes in training session
Homework—30 minutes

Exercise 17.7—60 to 90 minutes in training session

Materials

Peer Power, Book 2, Applying Peer Helper Skills (workbook), one copy for each trainee

Optional: If this module is used with an existing organization, one may want to use his/her own activities with which to work in Exercises 17.5, 17.6, and 17.7.

Introduction to Module

Many individuals who lack skills to do a good job are often called upon to serve in leadership roles. This is frustrating for the group and for the leader. This module will assist in helping trainees identify their own leadership styles and learn some practical ideas that will help them be an effective leader.

Training Procedures

1. Decide on grouping of the activities.

2. Decide if it is desired to use own organization.

3. Move from group to group to give feedback.

Evaluation Process

As a trainer, evaluate the process used in the teaching through feedback from participants and from the written work.

Measuring Outcomes

1. Use Exercise 17.1 to measure leadership style.

2. Use Exercises 17.2 and 17.3 to assess discussion group skills.

3. Use Exercise 17.4 to assess time management skills.

4. Use Exercises 17.5, 17.6, and 17.7 to actually set up a plan of action.

EXERCISE 17.1
LEADERSHIP STYLE PROFILE

Purpose

To help trainees assess their own leadership styles.

Introduction to Exercise

Leadership style is learned by individuals discovering the kind of leaders they are, either task-oriented or people-oriented. The following exercises will assist in reviewing the differences between the two.

Training Procedures

1. Discuss the different types of leaders: those that are democratic, laissez faire, and autocratic.

2. The leader may want to role-play the different types.

3. Have trainees fill out the "T-P Leadership Questionnaire."

4. Talk about the importance of combined concern for task and person.

5. Announce that to locate themselves on the "Leadership Style Profile" sheet, group participants will score their own questionnaires on the dimensions of task orientation (T) and people orientation (P).

6. Instruct the trainees in the scoring as follows:

   a. Circle the items number for items 8, 12, 17, 18, 19, 30, 34, and 35.

   b. Write a "1" in front of the circled items to which you responded S (seldom) or N (never).

   c. Write a "1" in front of items not circled to which you responded A (always) or F (frequently).

d. Count the circled "1's." This is your score for concern for people. Record this number in the blank following the letter "P."

e. Count the uncircled "1's." This is your score for concern for task. Record this number in the blank following the letter "T."

7. Ask trainee to follow directions on the profile sheet. Then lead a discussion of the implications that members attach to their location on the profile.

NOTE: The T-P Leadership Questionnaire comes from T.J. Sergiovanni, R. Metzcus, and L. Burden, (1969). Reprinted from *A Handbook of Structured Experiences for Human Relations Training, Volume I,* J. William Pfeiffer and John E. Jones, Editors, San Diego, CA. Copyright 1984, titled *"T-P Leadership Questionnaire: An Assessment of Style."*

Toward a particularistic approach to leadership style: Some findings. American Educational Research Journal, 6, 162-79.

Homework for Trainees after Group Meeting

1. Think about the types of leadership observed and decide if they are task oriented or people oriented.

2. Read the information in Exercise 17.2.

EXERCISE 17.2
LEADING A DISCUSSION GROUP

Purpose

To have the experience of leading a small discussion group and getting feedback.

Introduction to Exercise

Leaders are often asked to lead discussion groups. This exercise will assist the trainee in leading a discussion group.

Training Procedures

1. Ask for feedback from Exercise 17.1.
2. Have trainees divide into small discussion groups.
3. Ask one person to be an observer and use observation form.
4. Move among discussion groups and give leader feedback.
5. Continue until everyone has been both a discussion leader and an observer.

Homework for Trainees after Group Meeting

Look over Exercise 17.3.

EXERCISE 17.3 WORKING WITH OTHERS

Purpose

To assist the trainees in understanding how they relate to others who are different and can work with others who have different strengths. They also get practice in motivation others in a group meeting.

Introduction to Exercise

The ability to understand and work with others different from ourselves is an important skill to have and use. Individuals often withdraw and are afraid of individuals who are different. This exercise will take trainees through a role-play situation.

Training Procedures

1. Review previous homework.
2. Discuss the concept of individuals whom the trainees know who are different from them.
   a. Do they get along with them?
   b. Are they threatened?
3. Take the trainees first through an example of different types of individuals.
4. Lead a role-play with a group of different types of individuals.
5. Using the role-play example in *Peer Power, Book 2, Applying Peer Helper Skills* (workbook), the election, help them think of team members.

   Example: Outgoing individuals of different cultures. Someone good with accounting and money. Someone good at setting up an exact plan.
6. Have a group role-play the example. To do so will necessitate roles for each, including identifying the leader.
7. Following the role-playing, discuss the actions of the leader and help the group understand positive aspects and to identify other things that might have been done, if any.
8. Change roles so that all of the members have a chance to lead.

Homework for Trainees after Group Meeting

1. Have the trainees think of a group that they presently lead and decide how to work with those individuals who are different from themselves.
2. Have them prepare for the next exercise.

EXERCISE 17.4
TIME MANAGEMENT

Purpose

To help the trainees look at time wasters and look at how they spend their present time.

Introduction to Exercise

Often leaders are ineffective because they cannot get things done. This exercise will help you look at the time management skills of the trainees and suggest ways to change them.

Training Procedures

1. Discuss the different time wasters.

2. Discuss ways that they can change some of their time wasters.

3. Help the trainees look at the long-term and short-term goals that they have such as the following:

   Long-term goals

   - Going to college
   - Being a good parent
   - Becoming a pilot

   Short-term goals

   - Losing weight
   - Quitting smoking

4. Ask the trainees to make a list of activities for yesterday.

5. Ask them to account for the approximate time that it took.

6. Ask the trainees to indicate whether the activities were "have to" or "want to." Ask them to notice the balance.

7. Ask whether the activities fit into short-term or long-term goals.

8. Ask the trainees to develop a plan to manage their time differently.

Homework for Trainees after Group Meeting

1. Keep a chart of how you spend your time.

2. Keep a journal of how to change time problems.

3. Learn to prioritize activities.

4. Look for a balance of "have to" and "want to."

EXERCISE 17.5
DEVELOPING AN ACTION PLAN

Purpose

To assist trainees in developing their own action plan for a leadership position.

Introduction to Exercise

This activity will help trainees focus on how to establish what needs to be done in certain positions.

Training Procedures

1. Ask for feedback from Exercise 17.4.

2. Have the trainees work in groups of two to develop their own action plan.

3. If they do not have assigned leadership positions or cannot think of one, the trainer needs to assign one.

4. Work with the groups in the development of the plan.

5. Collect the action plans for written feedback.

Homework for Trainees after Group Meeting

If not done during the session, complete the action plan at home. Complete Exercise 17.6 for homework.

EXERCISE 17.6
PLANNING PUBLIC RELATIONS

Purpose

To assist trainees in following through with their plans for Exercise 17.5 and plan for the public relations aspect.

Introduction to Exercise

Leaders must keep their publics—membership, coworkers, community, organization officials—informed of plans, needs, and activities. To do so requires careful planning well in advance with responsibilities clearly delineated. Approval must be obtained before implementation of the plan, as well as assurance of financial and other necessary resources. The leader is the one to make sure that his public relations aspect is integrated early and throughout the action.

Training Procedures

1. Return material from Exercise 17.5 with comments. These sheets are to be used in Exercise 17.6.

2. Ask trainees to share homework from Exercise 17.6 and share comments that might help each other.

3. Divide the group so that they work in paris and ask them to assist each other in improving their public relations plans.

4. Demonstrate with a local specific example the different publics and their needs for different kinds of information about an organization or a business.
5. Collect the written plans.
6. Have trainees share experiences from working on their plans as partners and answer questions.

Homework for Trainees after Group Meeting

Complete Exercise 17.7 for next meeting.

EXERCISE 17.7
PLANNING A CONFERENCE OR OTHER MEETING

Purpose

To assist trainees to work as a team for planning a conference or meeting.

Introduction to Exercises

Leaders are often called upon to develop and plan a meeting. It is important to be able to do this.

Training Procedures

1. Return material from Exercise 17.6 and make comments.
2. Ask for any problem with homework from Exercise 17.7.
3. Ask trainees to share homework for Exercise 17.7 and make suggestions.
4. Ask trainees to divide into teams of three and plan the conference listed in *Peer Power, Book 2, Applying Peer Helping Skills* (workbook), or in their own area.
5. Collect the written plans.
6. Ask teams to share their plan with the entire training group. Offer suggestions.

MODULE **18**

PEER HELPING THROUGH TUTORING

Purpose

1. To learn material about motivation.
2. To understand their own ability to tutor.
3. To understand their own study habits.
4. To learn their own way of learning.
5. To learn specific ways of tutoring individuals in problem areas.
6. To learn how to deal with problem areas.
7. To learn how to be a successful tutor.

Approximate Time

Module 18—Introduction, 10 to 15 minutes for homework

Exercise 18.1—60 to 120 minutes
Homework—30 minutes

Exercise 18.2—30 to 60 minutes
Homework—30 minutes

Exercise 18.3—30 to 60 minutes
Homework—120 minutes

Exercise 18.4—120 to 160 minutes
Homework—120 minutes

Exercise 18.5—30 to 60 minutes
Homework—30 minutes

Exercise 16.6—60 to 120 minutes
Homework—30 minutes

Materials

Peer Power, Book 2, Applying Peer Helping Skills (workbook), one copy for each trainee

Optional: Slide, film, or video show on study skills

Speaker: Ask someone from special education (an L.D. or B.D. teacher).

Introduction to Module

Tutoring can be one of the most rewarding roles a peer can perform. I feel that it is very important that the peer tutor has completed *Peer Power, Book 1* before starting on this module. You may want to expand on this module if this is the only role that your trainees will be performing. You may want to include different material if they will be working with very young children or adults. The exercises and information from this unit also can be used with the tutee. The material is not designed to help tutors who are working with students with severe learning problems. These students may need professional tutors.

Training Procedures

1. Decide the number of training sessions and exercises to be included in this module.

2. Be prepared to demonstrate all the role-playing situations. If you don't feel comfortable, ask a professional teacher to demonstrate some of these role-playing situations.

3. If a speaker is used, time it with the appropriate exercise.

4. The homework portion of this module is important and should be reviewed carefully by you as the trainer.

5. When actually doing tutoring, the management becomes very important in terms of public relations with the cooperating teacher on such issues as the place to do the tutoring and support for the tutor and materials.

Evaluation Process

As a trainer, you can evaluate the process used in teaching a skill by the role-playing used by the trainees and the written homework.

Measuring Outcomes

1. Use Exercise 18.5 in terms of integration of skills.

2. Use Exercise 18.6 in terms of tutoring operation.

EXERCISE 18.1
SELF-ASSESSMENT

Purpose

1. To provide the trainees an opportunity to assess their own ability to tutor.

2. To review the introductory material.

Introduction to Exercise

The following assessment can be used before starting the module and at the conclusion. You may want to supplement the introduction section with a slide, film, or video show on motivation or learning.

Training Procedures

1. Review the material from the introduction as well as the reaction of the trainees to the slide, film, or video show.

2. Discuss motivation and Maslow's needs in relationship to where the trainees are as persons (e.g., level of love needs). Use the introduction material to Module 18, *Peer Power, Book 2, Applying Peer Helper Skills,* (workbook).

3. Discuss the difference between encouraging and discouraging statements.

4. Help the trainees complete the "Self-assessment Questionnaire" and look at the strengths that they have now as tutors.

5. Help the trainees set goals for improving weaknesses; use the entire group to brainstorm goals.

6. Have each trainee complete the goal sheet (last page of Exercise 18.1). Then talk with them individually and, when the plan is appropriate, sign the goal sheet to show your approval. (This may need to be completed at the next meeting with the group.)

Homework for Trainees after Group Meeting

1. Ask the trainees to fill out the goal skeet if not completed and review with them any additional ideas that you may have.

2. Have the trainees prepare for Exercise 18.2.

EXERCISE 18.2
HOW I STUDY

Purpose

1. To help the trainees understand their own study habits.
2. To help the trainees to develop a plan to improve their own study habits.

Introduction to Exercise

Discuss with the trainees that they need to understand their own values and their own ways of studying. Next they can use their strengths to help others, and they can learn new ways to study.

Trainees also may want to use this with their own tutee once a relationship has been established.

Training Procedures

1. Discuss the trainees' homework assignment.
2. Review the total scores on the "Personal Study Habits Survey."
3. Assist the trainees in seeing their strengths and weaknesses.
4. Assign homework to develop a plan (you may want to spend class time getting them started).

Homework for Trainees after Group Meeting

1. Develop a plan for change.
2. Bring back for review.
3. Prepare for Exercise 18.3.

EXERCISE 18.3
HOW I LEARN BEST

Purpose

1. To understand the preferred way of learning of each trainee.
2. To help the trainees apply this information to how they study.
3. To help the trainees apply this to the tutoring situation.

Introduction to Exercise

We all have a preferred way that we learn best. However, we need to develop additional learning styles. Be sure to be clear about these different learning styles and also about developing additional ways of learning. Use lecturer and/ or audio-visual materials.

Training Procedures

1. Use "Styles of Learning" found below in this exercise to use in your lecture about different styles of learning.
2. Provide examples and have the trainees brainstorm examples. Have them share how they learn.

   Examples

   - Big picture making
   - Making connection to something else
3. Have the trainees take and score the "Learning Style Survey."
4. Discuss the results of the survey.
5. Lead a discussion on "Discussion Questions."

6. Make the point that there is no right way to learn.

7. Work with the trainees, showing them how to do their homework.

Homework for Trainees after Group Meeting

1. Design and plan tutoring a person using each style.

2. Ask the trainees to use this skill in teaching various content areas.

3. Prepare for Exercise 18.4.

STYLES OF LEARNING

Visual Leaning. Learns by watching, likes to read, has good imagination, shows emotions facially, usually has neat penmanship, dresses neatly, plans and outlines, takes neat notes, like order and neatness.

Auditory Learning. Learns by listening, likes to discuss, remembers by reciting, will move lips while reading silently, likes quiet, is distracted by outside noise, displays emotion through intonation.

Kinesthetic Learning. Learns by doing, needs to be directly involved, likes to move around during study, appears impulsive, shows emotion, uses hands when talking, does not tend toward order and neatness.

Examples of visual tutoring:

- Write out an outline.
- Have tutees take notes

Examples of auditory tutoring:

- Read directions out loud.
- Talk to tutee about work.
- Tape record important things.

Examples of kinesthetic tutoring:

- Hands-on activity.
- Encourage writing.
- Trace new words.

EXERCISE 18.4
MAJOR STUDY SKILLS

Purpose

1. To teach the tutor how to use SQ3R method, test taking, note taking, writing skills, and time management.

2. To have the tutors practice using these skills.

Introduction to Exercise

This exercise may take three to four class periods to learn and practice. You may also want to invite a special education teacher to demonstrate some of these skills.

Training Procedures

1. Review the homework from the previous exercise.

2. Review the written material in this exercise.

3. Demonstrate each activity.

4. Have the trainees work in groups of three: one person is the tutor, one is the tutee, and one is the observer. The observer is to give feedback as to whether or not the tutor used the information in this exercise.

5. Have the trainees do the other activities identified in Directions 4 through 9.

Homework for Trainees after Group Meeting

Ask the tutors to write the activities that they were not able to complete in the group work.

Prepare for Exercise 18.5.

EXERCISE 18.5
PROBLEMS IN TUTORING

Purpose

1. To help the tutors learn how to deal with special problems in tutoring.

2. To practice using skills in tutoring.

Introduction to Exercise

This exercise needs to be used to integrate the skills used in *Peer Power, Book 1* and also in the earlier learning of this module.

Training Procedures

1. Review the homework.

2. Demonstrate the following:

   Attending
   Empathy
   Encouraging word
   Contracting

3. Ask the tutors to work in threes. As you observe their role-playing, ask them to work on attending, empathy, responses, encouragement, and contracting.

4. Stop after completing each of the directions in the *Peer Power, Book 2, Applying Peer Helper Skills* (workbook), and discuss and give feedback.

5. Lead a final discussion.

Homework for Trainees after Group Meeting

1. Have the trainees complete in writing those items in the directions that were not completed in the group.

2. Prepare for Exercise 18.6.

EXERCISE 18.6
PUTTING TUTORING SKILLS INTO ACTION

Purpose

1. To learn the steps involved in putting a tutoring program into action.

2. To practice skills of tutoring.

Introduction to Exercise

You may want to emphasize each of the points listed on each step and apply these to your local situation. Also trainees may want to take the self-assessment test again (Exercise 18.1).

Training Procedures

1. Review each of the steps.

2. Apply these to your local situation.

3. Demonstrate a tutoring experience.

4. Have the trainees divide into groups of three and practice tutoring. Have the observer fill out the observation sheet and share it with the trainee who then is to give it to you.

Homework for Trainees after Group Meetings

1. Set up a first meeting with cooperating teacher and tutee.

2. React to the role-playing situation.

3. Assign reading of the introduction to the next module.

MODULE **19**

FACILITATING SMALL DISCUSSION GROUPS

Purpose

To enable trainees to facilitate small discussion groups such as life problems groups (open-ended), subject matter groups (specific topic), and decision-making (problem-solving) groups (tasks).

Approximate Time

Module 19—Introduction
Homework—10 to 15 minutes

Exercise 19.1—30 to 40 minutes
Homework—40 minutes

Exercise 19.2—60 to 120 minutes
Homework—20 minutes

Exercise 19.3—60 to 90 minutes

Exercise 19.4—60 to 120 minutes
Homework—15 minutes

Exercise 19.5—60 to 120 minutes
Homework—15 minutes

Exercise 19.6—60 to 120 minutes
Homework—15 minutes

Materials

Peer Power, Book 2, Applying Peer Helper Skills (workbook), one copy for each trainee

Optional: If this module is used with an existing organization, you may want to use your own activities with which to work in Exercises 19.4, 19.5, and 19.6.

Introduction to Module

Many organizations have now gone to participatory management; therefore, facilitating group skills is essential. Many companies are using quality circles. Education is spending time with small discussion groups to use in terms of prevention and to help all participants feel that they belong. Churches are using the discussion format to assist their congregation to feel a part of the group and to make decisions.

Training Procedures

1. Decide on the exercises to use for this module.
2. Decide whether or not it is desirable to use your own organization issues.
3. Move from group to group to give feedback.
4. This could be used along with the Leadership Training Module 17.
5. Model each discussion before the trainees.
6. Once the peer counselors are trained in facilitating groups, design projects to use in small group work such as from elementary school age to adult to aging.

Evaluation Process

As a trainer, evaluate the process used in the teaching through the feedback obtained from the participants as well as by their written work and evaluation materials.

Measuring Outcomes

1. Use Exercise 19.4 to measure skills in the life problems group (facilitating open-ended discussions).

2. Use Exercise 19.5 to measure skills in the subject matter group (facilitating discussions on specific topics).

3. Use Exercise 19.6 to measure skills in the decision-making (problem-solving) group (facilitating discussions related to tasks).

EXERCISE 19.1
SELF-ASSESSMENT OF GROUP FACILITATOR SKILLS

Purpose

To help trainees assess their own group facilitator skills.

Introduction to Exercise

Group facilitation skills are difficult and involve skills first in basic communication. The following exercise will assist trainees in reviewing their own perception of basic skills.

Training Procedures

1. Discuss each of the areas being assessed and give examples.

2. Mention the following as basic conditions for a good small group discussion:

a. Clear topic of interest to the group.

b. Group members who differ in their opinions.

c. A climate of acceptance so as to promote expression.

d. A facilitator who gets things going and then serves as a guide.

3. Have the trainees take assessment.

4. Discuss each area and gain ideas from the trainees.

5. Have the group members share their strengths and weaknesses.

Homework for Trainees after Group Meeting

1. Help the participants find groups in which to participate as homework.

2. Prepare for Exercise 19.2.

EXERCISE 19.2
FUNCTIONS OF A DISCUSSION FACILITATOR

Purpose

To help the trainees to understand the different functions and activities involved in leading a group and also to practice on small activities.

Introduction to Exercise

Peer counselors are often asked to facilitate small discussion groups. Before leading an entire group, it is good to practice on small segments of group facilitation.

Training Procedures

1. Review all of the functions. Use the list provided in "Group Facilitator Functions" listed in *Peer Power, Book 2, Applying Peer Helper Skills* (workbook).

2. Place the functions on chalkboard or flipchart.

3. Have a discussion around each area.

4. Demonstrate as a leader each section.

   Example: Dealing with problem participants. (Number 5 in the "Group Facilitator Functions" list).

5. Have the trainees move into groups of four with one observer, and have the facilitator of each group lead the group on just one issue (e.g., starting a group). Have the observer use the feedback form entitled "Discussion Skills Observations." Then have the observer give feedback. Make sure that each group works on all of the issues. Rotate roles in the group.

Homework for Trainees after Group Meeting

1. Examine checklist from Exercise 19.1.

2. Prepare for Exercise 19.3.

EXERCISE 19.3
LEADING A DISCUSSION GROUP

Purpose

To provide the trainees with the experience of leading a small discussion group and getting feedback.

Introduction to Exercise

Leaders are often asked to facilitate a discussion group. This exercise will assist the trainee in facilitating a discussion group.

Training Procedures

1. Ask for feedback from Exercise 19.2.
2. Demonstrate what you are asking the trainees to do.
3. Have the trainees divide into small discussion groups.
4. Ask one person to be an observer and use the "Observer Evaluation Form."
5. Move among discussion groups and give feedback to the facilitator.
6. Continue until everyone has been both a discussion leader and an observer.

Homework for Trainees after Group Meeting

1. Look over Exercise 19.1.
2. Prepare for Exercise 19.4

EXERCISE 19.4
LIFE PROBLEMS GROUP

Purpose

To have the trainees experience leading a rap group (life problems group).

Introduction to Exercise

One of the most valuable benefits of participating in a peer counseling group is the sharing that takes place. This exercise will give participants an opportunity to share their own concerns or some from the stimulus questions entitled "Let's Discuss."

Training Procedures

1. Ask for feedback from the previous exercise.
2. Review the role of facilitator in this type of group.
3. Demonstrate a life problems group.
4. Divide into groups of five, with one being the facilitator, one the observer, and three the participants.
5. Have the observer focus on facilitator skills using the "Group Feedback Form" provided. You may want to have the observer give the "Group Feedback Form" to the facilitator who in turn will give it to you.

Homework for Trainees after Group Meeting

1. Have the participants refer back to the skills listed in Exercise 19.1 and evaluate their own effectiveness.
2. Prepare for Exercise 19.5.

EXERCISE 19.5
SUBJECT MATTER GROUP

Purpose

To train facilitators to present topical groups.

Introduction to Exercise

Often information that is presented by peers is far more accepted by the group members than that presented by the group leader; therefore, it would be helpful for your peer group facilitators to have various topics that they can discuss.

Training Procedures

1. Ask for feedback from Exercise 19.4.

2. Demonstrate leading a group before asking the trainees to lead a group.

3. Have the trainees divide into small discussion groups.

4. Ask one person to be a discussion facilitator and another person to be an observer and use observation form.

5. Move among discussion groups and give the facilitator feedback.

6. Continue until everyone has been both a discussion facilitator and an observer.

7. Focus on the group members.

Homework for Trainees after Group Meeting

1. Look over Exercise 19.1.

2. Prepare for Exercise 19.6.

EXERCISE 19.6
DECISION-MAKING GROUP

Purpose

To help the trainees with experience in leading a small group that needs to perform a task or arrive at a solution.

Introduction to Exercise

Facilitators are asked to help groups make decisions and solve problems. This exercise will assist the trainee with this type of group.

Training Procedures

1. Ask for feedback from Exercise 19.2.

2. Review the steps to problem solving (as outlined in Module 12, *Peer Power, Book 1),* and spend time having trainees discuss and understand brainstorming (see the section on "Brainstorming" in *Peer Power, Book 2* [workbook], Exercise 19.6).

3. Demonstrate a problem-solving group.

4. Have the trainees divide into small discussion groups and use one of the "Suggested Decisions to Be Made" or one that you give them.

5. Ask one person to be an observer and use observation form.

6. Move among discussion groups and give the facilitator feedback.

7. Continue until everyone has been both a discussion leader and an observer.

Homework for Trainees after Group Meeting

1. Look over Exercise 19.1.

2. Prepare for Exercise 20.1.

MODULE **20**

LEADING CLASSROOM GROUPS

Purpose

1. To enable trainees to learn some introductory material concerning leading classroom groups.

2. To become aware of the different skills needed to lead a classroom group.

3. To give trainees practice in leading classroom groups.

Approximate Time

Module 20—Introduction
Homework—30 to 45 minutes.

Exercise 20.1—30 to 60 minutes
Homework—20 minutes for one week

Exercise 20.2—60 to 90 minutes
Homework—60 minutes

Exercise 20.3—30 to 60 minutes
Homework—30 minutes

Exercise 20.4—90 to 120 minutes
Homework—60 minutes

Exercise 20.5—60 minutes
Homework—30 minutes

Exercise 20.6—4 to 5 hours
Homework—60 minutes

Materials

Peer Power, Book 2, Applying Peer Helper Skills (workbook), one copy for each trainee

Introduction to Module

Peer helpers are often asked to lead classroom groups on various topics. Research supports the idea that health issues when presented by peers have more impact than when presented by professional teachers. Therefore an appropriate activity for peer counselors is classroom groups. It is suggested that the supervisor monitor closely the content of each lesson for accuracy. A good idea also is to have a professional in the classroom during the presentation.

Training Procedures

1. Decide the number of training sessions and exercises to be included in each.

2. Review the content to be covered as well as the suggested activities, as listed in *Peer Power, Book 2, Applying Peer Helper Skills* (workbook).

3. Be prepared to demonstrate what you are asking the trainees to do.

4. Be prepared to offer lots of suggestions on developing classroom activities.

5. Decide whether or not you want to use your own classroom lessons on which the trainees might practice.

6. Help the trainees in the planning phase.

7. If you choose, use this exercise along with Module 19, "Facilitating Small Discussion Groups."

8. Once the peer counselors are trained in leading large groups, design projects to use with large groups. For example use with community groups or with elementary, middle, and high school classes on health issues, value clarification, and so forth.

9. Have a professional present when a peer counselor is leading a class.

Evaluation Process

As a trainer, you can evaluate the learning based on the homework that the trainees hand in and also by observing them in their role-play activities.

Measuring Outcomes

1. Use Exercise 10.1 before and after the module to check for understanding.

2. Use the observation form from Exercise 20.6 to check on skill developing.

3. Watch and listen closely during the role-playing to measure the ease with which the trainees are able to do this skill.

EXERCISE 20.1
CHECKLIST OF SKILLS FOR CLASSROOM GROUP

Purpose

To learn some of the skills needed for leading a classroom group as compared to one-on-one helping and small group discussion.

Introduction to Exercise

In Exercise 20.1, the trainees will learn the differences among skills needed for a variety of helping roles. They also will become aware of the skills they need to improve.

Training Procedures

1. Discuss the introductory material.

2. Have the trainees review together the "Skills of Helping" chart and discuss each point.

3. Have the trainees particularly take note of those skills unique to a large classroom.

4. Have the trainees mark for each skill whether it is a strength, possessed and feel comfortable in using, or need help to develop.

5. Have each trainee identify possible ways other members of the group might assist him or her in developing one or more of the areas.

Homework for Trainees after Group Meeting

Ask the trainees to write a plan of action to improve those areas that need developing.

EXERCISE 20.2
UNDERSTANDING OTHERS

Purpose

To assist trainees in understanding that different learning styles exist in the classroom and that provision for all of the styles need to be considered.

Introduction to Exercise

Any learning situation for all of us depends on the teacher and the learner and the interaction between the two. You as leader need to make sure that some of the activities in the lesson are designed for different types of learning styles.

Training Procedures

1. Discuss the homework from the previous exercise.

2. Preview the appropriate material from the tutoring module. (Number 18).

3. Ask the trainees to complete the "Different Ways to Learn" chart.

4. Have the entire group share so that all areas are covered (put on the board).

5. Brainstorm additional ways of teaching different styles.

Homework for Trainees after Group Meeting

Ask the trainees to give activity examples of how they would teach a group on "How to Cook Breakfast." Make sure that they have a variety of activities, appealing to different kinds of learning.

EXERCISE 20.3
MOTIVATING OTHERS

Purpose

To understand what motivates us as well as others in terms of learning.

Introduction to Exercise

Motivation is very difficult to understand and trainees will need to recognize this so as not to get discouraged as they try to motivate others. Help trainees understand what motivates them as well as others.

Training Procedures

1. Review the homework from the previous exercise.

2. Lead the group through the "Visualization Exercise".

VISUALIZATION EXERCISE

   a. Play soft music in the background (e.g., Steve Halern tapes).

   b. Have each person get very comfortable.

   c. Relax each part of the body (take them through each body part). Use a visualizing exercise from a book or use a visualizing tape if you have not previously gained proficiency in this exercise.

   d. Imagine a very quiet place that is special (e.g., mountain, ocean).

   e. Imagine that you are learning a new task.

      (1) What got you excited?

      (2) What is happening?

      (3) What was the thing that the leader did that helped you to learn?

      (4) Open your eyes and feel refreshed and relaxed.

3. Have the participants draw and/or write the scene in their images.

4. Discuss the image with the entire group.

5. Write motivator on the board.

6. Get the group to brainstorm examples of motivator.

Homework for Trainees after Group Meeting

1. Have the trainees think of motivating activities for teaching others how to get along with their peers.

2. Prepare for Exercise 20.4.

EXERCISE 20.4
PUBLIC SPEAKING SKILLS

Purpose

To teach specific skills in public speaking.

Introduction to Exercise

This exercise is not meant to be a complete class in speech. It is designed to focus on specific skills needed for large groups.

Training Procedures

1. Review the homework from the previous exercise.

2. Review the "Public Speaking Skills" listed in *Peer Power, Book 2, Applying Peer Helper Skills* (workbook), as well as others that you think are important.

3. Have the trainees give a five-minute talk on something about which they know a lot. They may use notes.

4. Ask the audience to give feedback concerning public speaking skills. They may use the "Public Speaking Skills" list.

Homework for Trainees after Group Meeting

1. Ask the trainees to practice in front of a mirror and look at their nonverbal behavior as they talk.

2. Prepare for Exercise 20.5.

EXERCISE 20.5
PLANNING FOR LARGE GROUPS

Purpose

To learn some of the skills needed in planning a lesson.

Introduction to Exercise

If a large group lesson goes well, most frequently the reason is because the leader is organized and has a lesson plan. The art of planning is difficult. Once you have a plan, it is much easier to change it if things are not going well than to have no plan at all.

Training Procedures

1. Review the homework from the previous exercise.
2. Review the steps needed to be taken for planning a lesson.
3. Have the trainees work in triads to design a classroom presentation on "Good Listening Skills."
4. Work with each of the groups to assist in their thinking and planning.
5. Have someone from each group share their lesson plan with the entire group.

Homework for Trainees after Group Meeting

1. Refine the lesson plan.
2. Prepare for Exercise 20.6.

EXERCISE 20.6
PRACTICE IN LARGE CLASSROOM GROUP PRESENTATION

Purpose

To provide practice in leading a classroom group with a set lesson.

Introduction to Exercise

To decide how long each activity will take and actually have all of the materials available is a difficult task. Using the two examples included in this exercise, allow each trainee to lead the other trainees in the activity.

Training Procedures

1. Review the homework.
2. Go over the two sample classroom exercises provided in the *Peer Power, Book 2, Applying Peer Helper Skills* (workbook) and demonstrate.
3. Divide into groups of 4 or 5 members each.
4. Have each person present one of the lessons for the rest of the group.
5. Have one person play the observer role and give the leader feedback.

Homework for Trainees after Group Meeting

1. Read the introduction to the next module.
2. Prepare for Exercise 21.1.

MODULE **21**

RECOGNIZING EATING DISORDER PROBLEMS

Purposes

1. To learn about eating disorders.

2. To become aware of their own potential for having an eating disorder.

3. To learn signs of eating disorders in others.

4. To learn some intervention techniques for dealing with a person with an eating disorder.

Approximate Time

Module 21—Introduction, 30 minutes for homework

Exercise 21.1—30 to 60 minutes
Homework—30 minutes for one week

Exercise 21.2—30 to 60 minutes
Homework—30 minutes

Exercise 21.3—60 minutes
Homework—30 minutes

Exercise 21.4—30 to 60 minutes
Homework—30 minutes

Exercise 21.5—60 to 120 minutes
Homework—30 minutes

Exercise 21.6—60 minutes
Homework—20 minutes

Exercise 21.7—60 minutes
Homework—15 minutes

Materials

Optional: Filmstrip, film, or other audio-visual material on eating disorders.

Optional: Pamphlets from some of the references.

Speaker: Ask someone from an eating disorder program or from OverEaters Anonymous to come and talk with the group.

Books

Bauer, Anderson, & Hyatt. *Bulimia; Book for Therapist and Client.* (1986). Accelerated Development Inc., 3808 W. Kilgore Avenue, Muncie, IN 47304-4896.

Hollis. *Fat Is a Family Affair.* Hazelden.

Stein & Unell. *Anorexia Nervosa.* Comp Care Publications.

Introduction to Module

Eating disorders are on the rise in this country. Anorexia, bulimia, and compulsive overeating are dangerous illnesses that need intervention. Eating disorders are progressive, addictive diseases in that the behaviors become very compulsive and generally get worse before getting better. Multiple interventions are needed for individuals suffering from eating disorders, sometimes hospitalization, and sometimes outpatient help. Generally the involvement of a dietitian, psychiatrist, medical doctor, dentist, and psychologist are needed in the treatment of eating disorders. This module, along with "Stress Management—Moving toward Wellness," Module 15, might be taught together. You will need to help the peer counselors learn that they must refer to a professional mental health person if they encounter this problem rather than trying to handle this themselves. Exercises from the module can be used in the classroom presentations and/or small group discussions.

Filmstrip, films, other audio-visual material, and speakers may be used with this module.

Training Procedures

1. Decide the number of training sessions and exercises to be included in this module.

2. Review the content to be covered as well as the suggested activities, as listed in *Peer Power, Book 2, Applying Peer Helper Skills* (workbook).

3. Be prepared to do a role-playing or videotape of a person with an eating disorder.

4. If a speaker is to be used, the trainer may want to schedule this early in the training.

5. It might be helpful to have the peer helpers order materials from the resources listed at the end of Exercise 21.6.

6. Ask the peer helpers to keep a journal of food intake and also complete their homework assignments.

Evaluation Process

As a trainer, you can evaluate the process used in teaching a skill through the feedback obtained from trainees and by observation of their written work as well as their behavior when practicing the skills during training sessions.

Measuring Outcomes

1. So that trainees might assess their own eating disorder, use Exercise 21.1.

2. Use Exercise 21.3 so that the trainees might judge where they are as a person with eating disorders or as an enabler.

3. Watch and listen closely during the role-playing in Exercise 21.6 to measure the ease with which trainees are using the techniques learned earlier in the module and skills of empathy and confrontation. You may want to have helpers tape record their role-playing and use the tapes for your evaluation process.

EXERCISE 21.1
FOOD CHART

Purposes

1. To provide the trainees an opportunity to keep a food chart.

2. To review introductory material.

Introduction to Exercise

In the introduction of Module 21, the trainees will learn some facts about eating disorders. This would be a good time to show a film or listen to a lecture.

In this exercise the trainees will get in touch with their own eating patterns.

1. Review the material from the introduction as well as the reaction of the trainees to film or speaker.

2. Discuss the material in terms of whether or not the trainees agree with it.

3. Have the trainees keep a food chart for a week.

4. Have the trainees chart their food from yesterday and walk them through the chart.

5. Ask the trainees what they have learned so far from the food chart and the material that they have read.

6. Ask the trainees how they might change their eating behavior.

Homework for Trainees after Group Meeting

1. Ask the trainees to keep during this whole module a journal of their homework assignments.

2. Ask the trainees to keep a "Food Intake Chart" and bring it in each day of training.

3. Prepare for Exercise 21.2.

EXERCISE 21.2
ASSESSING EATING DISORDERS

Purpose

To provide an opportunity for trainees to examine their own risk for eating disorders and also to recognize eating disorder problems in others.

Introduction to Exercise

As individuals become aware of their own eating disorder risk, many will begin to get professional help to reduce that problem. As peer helpers recognize these risk factors in others they will refer them to professional counselors. What has been found is that often peer helpers are the first to recognize eating problems; hopefully they would refer the person with the problem for professional help.

Training Procedures

1. Discuss the trainees' homework from the previous exercise and review the goals that they have set.

2. Have the trainees answer yes or no to the "Self-assessment Checklist on Eating Disorders."

3. Ask the trainees to share their information from the check list with the group.

4. Have the group members assist each other in suggesting intervention strategies to reduce eating problems.

5. Ask the trainees to think of someone they know and try to assess their potential for an eating disorder.

Homework for Trainees after Group Meeting

1. Have the trainees continue with their journal.

2. Ask them to write in their journal their reactions to their eating behavior.

3. Prepare for Exercise 21.3.

EXERCISE 21.3
BULIMIA, ANOREXIA, COMPULSIVE OVEREATING:
WHERE ARE YOU AS AN EATING DISORDERED PERSON OR ENABLER?

Purposes

1. To help trainees understand that an eating disorder is a progressive disorder.

2. To help trainees understand the concept of co-dependency in eating disorders.

Introduction to Exercise

An eating disorder is a progressive, addictive disease. The behaviors associated with eating are addictive. Unlike alcoholism or chemical dependency, one cannot stop eating.

Therefore it is important to examine where the individual is on the disease chart. It is also important to look at the issue of co-dependency and see whether or not the person with an eating disorder is a co-dependent to someone else.

Training Procedures

1. Review the homework journal and food chart from the two previous exercises and discuss these.
2. Review the two charts in *Peer Power, Book 2, Applying Peer Helper Skills* (workbook).
3. Review co-dependency. If done in the group, skill must be used because of effect upon those trainees who are co-dependents or are close to someone who is.
4. Discuss ways to get out of the co-dependency.

Homework for Trainees after Group Meeting

1. Ask the trainees to continue keeping their food charts and journals.
2. Focus on items in Directions 2 through 5.

EXERCISE 21.4
FOOD CHOICE EVALUATION

Purpose

To learn about the four food groups and learn whether or not the trainees are eating food from the four food groups.

Introduction to Exercise

The four food groups are important to know and to be a guide to healthy eating. You may want to have a dietitian talk before this activity.

Training Procedures

1. Review the homework from the previous exercise.
2. Ask the trainees to bring in their food charts and use the information for the last full day.
3. Put the information from the food chart of the "Food Record" and follow directions on food choice evaluation.
4. Review the "Food Selection Changes" and help the trainees set goals for healthy eating.

Homework for Trainees after Group Meeting

1. Have the trainees do their homework based on suggested questions from the book and continue with the food charts.
2. Prepare for Exercise 21.5.

EXERCISE 21.5
CULTURAL IMPACT ON EATING DISORDERS

Purpose

To help the trainees to understand the cultural impact on eating problems and understand self-worth and body image.

Introduction to Exercise

Men and women are influenced by the media (TV, magazines, billboards), and the relationship between the media and real individuals is very limited, if any.

Training Procedures

1. Review the homework.
2. Allow plenty of time for this activity and bring in popular magazines for both men and women.

3. Ask the trainees to look at billboards and TV commercials.

4. As they are looking at pictures in the magazines, as trainer, point out certain pictures that make the point of the difference between media and real individuals at work, supermarkets, and so forth.

5. Have a discussion on cultural push for thinness and fitness and how this affects individuals' self-esteem.

6. If possible, have the trainees work at an art table cutting out pictures and putting on poster boards with glue. Make sure you have enough poster board and glue for all the participants.

7. Have the trainees to make a collage to describe themselves.

8. Ask each person to present their collage to the rest of the group and have them to explain their collage.

9. Discuss at the end how much emphasis is on beauty, body size, and so forth.

Homework for Trainees after Group Meeting

1. Ask the trainees to turn in an essay at the next training meeting concerning how they view the impact of culture on eating behaviors.

2. Ask the trainees to react to the collage, would they like to be different?

EXERCISE 21.6
PRACTICE IN HELPING A PERSON WITH AN EATING DISORDER

Purposes

1. To help the trainees to learn intervention techniques for coping with another person with an eating disorder.

2. To help the trainees to learn that they must refer to a professional(s).

Introduction to Exercise

Stress that an eating disorder is a serious issue for peer helpers to deal with and that they must obtain additional help if the person they are dealing with is an eating disorder candidate.

Training Procedures

1. Review and discuss the homework journal from the previous exercise.

2. Review materials learned earlier.

3. Review skills of attending, empathy, questioning, and confrontation.

4. Review observer role.

5. Demonstrate role-play first.

6. Ask participants to work together in groups of three.

7. Move from group to group assessing helpers.

Homework for Trainees after Group Meeting

1. Ask the trainees to continue writing in their journal

2. Assign outside reading if available.

3. Have the peer counselor get local information concerning help for eating disorders.

4. Prepare for Exercise 21.7.

EXERCISE 21.7
LOOKING AT MYSELF

Purposes

1. To examine how the individual trainees view themselves in relation to all the material they have learned and have been writing about.

2. To set goals for the future.

Introduction to Exercise

Review all the learning and talk about eating disorders being multidimensional.

Training Procedures

1. Have the trainees complete Direction 1 and help them to discuss each one with you and participants.

2. Assist trainees to set new goals relative to their eating behavior and exercise behavior.

3. Have the trainees share their goals with the group.

4. Collect the journals and respond to writing of the trainees.

5. Use the journal for evaluation.

Homework for Trainees after Group Meeting

1. Read the information in first part of Module 22.

2. Prepare for Exercise 22.1.

MODULE **22**

SUICIDE PREVENTION

Purposes

1. To learn some information about suicide.

2. To become aware of their own potential for suicide.

3. To learn signs of potential suicide in others.

4. To learn some intervention techniques for others considering suicide.

Approximate Time

Module 22—Introduction
Homework—10 to 15 minutes

Explaining the program—30 to 45 minutes

Exercise 22.1—30 to 60 minutes
Homework—30 to 60 minutes

Exercise 22.2—30 to 60 minutes
Homework—30 to 60 minutes

Exercise 22.3—30 to 60 minutes
Homework—20 minutes

Exercise 22.4—60 to 90 minutes
Homework—10 minutes

Exercise 22.5—60 minutes
Homework—30 to 60 minutes

Materials

Peer Power, Book 2, Applying Peer Helper Skills (workbook), one for each trainee

Optional: Slide show on suicide. "Preventing Teenage Suicide: You can Help" or "Teenage Blues: Coping with Depression," Sunburst Communications.

Optional: Pamphlets from some of the suicide prevention organizations.

Speaker: From a hospice unit or a suicide prevention center.

Book: Rosenthal, Howard. *Now with My Life I Don't.* Accelerated Development Inc., 3808 W. Kilgore Avenue. Muncie, Indiana 47304-4896.

Introduction to Module

Suicide was an epidemic in the 80s and continues to be prevalent in the 90s. It is very common these days for all individuals to know of someone who has committed suicide or who has attempted suicide. Apparently this approach to dealing with stress is becoming an alternative. Many persons have a difficult time coping with stress in a healthy manner. Peer helpers need to understand clearly that, should they run into this problem, rather than trying to handle it themselves, they must refer the individual to a professional. This module might be taught along with "Stress Management—Moving toward Wellness" (Module 15).

Audio-visual materials and speakers may be used with this module.

Training Procedures

1. Decide the number of training sessions and exercises to be included in this module.

2. Review the content to be covered, as well as the suggested activities, as listed in *Peer Power, Book 2, Applying Peer Helper Skills* (workbook).

3. Be prepared to do a role-playing or videotape of a suicidal person.

4. If a speaker is to be used, the trainer may want to schedule this early in the training.

5. Suggest that peer counselors order material from the resources listed.

6. Ask peer counselors to keep a reaction journal throughout this module.

Evaluation Process

As a trainer, you can evaluate the process used in teaching a skill through the feedback obtained from trainees and by observation of their written work as well as their behavior when practicing the skills during training sessions.

Measuring Outcomes

1. So that the trainees might find their own stress level, use Exercise 22.1.

2. Use Exercise 22.2 so that the trainees might judge their own vulnerability to suicide.

3. Watch and listen closely during the role-playing in Exercise 22.5 to measure the ease with which trainees are using the techniques of intervention learned in Exercise 22.3.

EXERCISE 22.1
HOW STRESSFUL ARE YOU?

Purposes

1. To provide the trainees an opportunity to assess their own stress level.

2. To review introductory material.

Introduction to Exercise

In the introduction of Module 22, the trainees will learn some facts about suicide. This would be a good time to show a filmstrip.

In this exercise the trainees will learn their own level of stress.

Training Procedures

1. Review the material from the introduction as well as the reaction of the trainees to the filmstrip.

2. Discuss the material in terms of whether or not the trainees agree with it.

3. Have the trainees take "The Teen Scene: Stress Test."

4. Discuss their own results and what these results mean to the trainees.

5. As a group, use brainstorming techniques for reducing stress in the lives of the trainees.

6. Ask the trainees to set some goals to deal with stress.

Homework for Trainees after Group Meeting

1. Ask the trainees to keep during this whole module a journal on their feelings and reactions to the discussion on suicide.

2. Ask the trainees specifically to focus on a plan to deal with their own stress level based on their score on "The Teen Scene: Stress Test."

3. Ask them to write some goal(s) to deal with stress in their lives.

EXERCISE 22.2
SUICIDE RISKS

Purpose

To provide an opportunity for trainees to examine their own risk for suicide and also to recognize suicide risk in others.

Introduction to Exercise

As individuals become aware of their own suicide risk many will begin to get professional help to reduce that risk. As peer counselors recognize these risk factors in others they will refer them to professional counselors. It has been found that once peer counselors are trained to recognize these risk factors, many of the referrals to professional counselors become more serious.

Training Procedures

1. Discuss their homework from previous exercise and review the goals set up by the trainees.

2. Have the trainees look over the list of possible suicide risk factors.

3. Ask the trainees to share their score with the group.

4. Have the trainees assist each other in suggesting intervention strategies to reduce risk factors.

5. Ask the trainees to think of someone they know and try to assess their potential for suicide.

Homework for Trainees after Group Meeting

1. Continue with the trainees' journal.

2. Ask the trainees to write a plan to reduce their own potential for suicide.

3. Ask the trainees to think of someone they know who has several risk factors and plan an intervention to get professional help.

4. Prepare for Exercise 22.3.

EXERCISE 22.3
INTERVENTION TECHNIQUES

Purposes

1. To help trainees learn intervention techniques for coping with a potential suicide candidate.

2. To help trainees learn that they must refer to professionals.

Introduction to Exercise

The trainer must stress that this is a serious issue for peer helpers to deal with and that they must get additional help if the person with whom they are dealing is a suicide candidate.

Training Procedures

1. Review the homework journal from the previous exercise and discuss it.

2. Review intervention techniques, discuss them in the group, and help participants explore additional techniques.

3. Identify those techniques with which the trainees agree and disagree.

4. Brainstorm with the entire group a plan of action in dealing with a potentially suicidal person.

5. have trainees to develop a resource list of professional people and materials for their use in working with suicidal persons and/or those affected by a suicide.

Homework for Trainees after Group Meeting

1. Have the trainees continue writing in the journal.
2. Assign outside reading if available.
3. Prepare for Exercise 22.4.

EXERCISE 22.4 ASSISTING THOSE LEFT TO LIVE ON AFTER A SUICIDE

Purposes

1. To assist trainees in understanding impact of suicide on others.
2. To assist trainees in setting up a plan to assist survivors.

Introduction to Exercise

This might be a good exercise for which to have a speaker, perhaps from a hospice or suicide prevention group. The issue of dealing with loss using Kubler-Ross material on grieving may be very appropriate for this exercise. Depending on the population served by the peer counselors (e.g., school, hospital, business), they may want to come up with a plan should a suicide happen.

Training Procedures

1. Review the journal from the previous exercise.
2. Review "Stages of Loss"; show a filmstrip if appropriate or have a speaker.

3. Discuss how the peer counselor would assist a survivor.

4. Discuss a plan for the local community if a suicide were to happen how could the peer counselors assist the survivors?

Homework for Trainees after Group Meeting

1. Have trainees to write how they might react to helping a survivor of suicide if this wasn't completed before class ended.

2. Write what they believe their thoughts and feelings would be if they were to lose someone close to them to suicide.

3. Prepare for Exercise 22.5.

EXERCISE 22.5
PRACTICE IN HELPING A SUICIDAL PERSON

Purposes

1. To help trainees practice helping a suicidal person.

2. To help trainees role-play getting the potential helpee to a professional.

Introduction to Exercise

Peer helpers are often put in the position of being aware that someone is considering suicide, and they sometimes try to handle it themselves. This hopefully will help them learn the skills needed to get an individual to seek professional help. Each role-play may last 20 to 30 minutes if they are using their basic skills (e.g., attending, empathy, questioning) and advanced intervention techniques. They may want to use for their own role that they have made up for practice.

Training Procedures

1. Demonstrate the following role-play using information from the previous exercises, introduction material, and the skills from *Peer Power, Book 1.*

   Potential Suicide Victims: This is a white male, an excellent student, and a perfectionist. The boy slashed his wrist earlier this year when a good friend was killed in a car wreck. He has few friends and recently has been very depressed. To deal with depression, he has started drinking on the weekends.

2. Divide the class into groups of three and role-play a potential suicide victim, a helper, and an observer. Change roles until all have had a chance to play all three roles.

3. The observer should use the forms in the exercises containing guides for the observer.

4. Discuss the trainees' reactions to all roles.

Homework for Trainees after Group Meeting

1. Ask the trainees to write in their journal their feelings about this activity.

2. Ask the trainees to request information from referral sources (list was developed in Exercise 22.3).

3. Ask the trainees to turn in their journals following this exercise.

4. Use the journal for evaluation.

5. Prepare for Module 23 and Exercise 23.1.

MODULE **23**

COPING WITH LOSS

Purposes

1. To learn about loss.
2. To help trainees understand how they deal with loss.
3. To understand grieving.
4. To practice helping others cope with loss.

Approximate Time

Module 23—Introduction—10 minutes

Exercise 23.1—60 minutes
Homework—30 minutes

Exercise 23.2—60 minutes
Homework—30 minutes

Exercise 23.3—60 minutes
Homework—30 minutes

Exercise 23.4—60 to 90 minutes
Homework—30 minutes

Materials

Peer Power, Book 2, Applying Peer Helper Skills (workbook), one copy for each trainee

Optional: Slide show or film on death and dying.

Speaker: Ask someone from a hospice unit.

Introduction to Module

This module can be very emotional for the group members. A high level of trust and skills is needed when you do this module. You may need to spend additional time with this module than that which is suggested.

Training Procedures

1. Decide the number of training sessions and exercises to be included in this module.

2. Review the content to be covered and the suggested activities as listed in *Peer Power, Book 2, Applying Peer Helper Skills* (workbook).

3. Be prepared to share your own loss and how you coped with it.

4. You might want a speaker to come into the group.

Evaluation Process

As a trainer, you can evaluate the process used in teaching a skill by the feedback obtained from the trainees and by observation of their written work and behavior when practicing a skill.

Measuring Outcomes

1. Use Exercise 23.4 to review skills.

2. Use written homework.

EXERCISE 23.1
MY OWN LOSSES

Purpose

To look at one's own loss and how one coped.

Introduction to Exercise

This exercise can be very powerful. It is important that you give enough time for the exercise as well as time to discuss it.

Training Procedures

1. Discuss with the trainees the loss line.
2. Show them an example.
3. Have them draw "My Age-Loss Line." If this is to be shared with the total group, use newsprint or poster board.
4. Ask them to share their loss line within a small group or with the group.
5. Discuss how they coped.
6. Point out the impact if too many losses were to occur too close together.

Homework for Trainees after Group Meeting

1. Have the trainees write down their reaction to the exercise.
2. Prepare for Exercise 23.2.

EXERCISE 23.2
TYPES OF LOSS

Purpose

To learn the types of loss encountered by the trainees and how they coped.

Introduction to Exercise

We all have dealt with loss at some time in our lives. How did we cope with it, and did formal rituals help?

Training Procedures

1. Discuss the exercise and have the trainees list their losses and identify ways of coping.

2. This would be a good exercise during which to show a film or have a speaker on rituals of loss—formal (Funerals) and informal (talking).

3. Explain rituals, formal and informal, and give examples.

4. Discuss the activity with the group.

Homework for Trainees after Group Meeting

1. Write in your journal your reaction to this exercise with an emphasis on coping.

2. Prepare for Exercise 23.3.

EXERCISE 23.3
THE GRIEVING PROCESS

Purpose

To help the trainees understand the grieving process.

Introduction to Exercise

In this exercise the trainees will learn the grieving process and where they are in reference to their own grieving.

Training Procedures

1. Review the grieving process.

2. Lead a discussion on where each person is with the grieving process.

3. Explore with them the different feelings that they have at different stages.

4. Have a discussion on how can this knowledge be helpful in working with others.

Homework for Trainees after Group Meeting

1. Write in your journal your reaction to the grieving process.

2. Prepare for Exercise 23.4.

EXERCISE 23.4 OFFERING SUPPORT TO OTHERS

Purpose

To provide practice in helping individuals with the loss process.

Introduction to Exercise

Often individuals are uncomfortable talking about loss. This exercise will help the trainees to be able to listen to others about their loss.

Training Procedures

1. Review "The Grieving Process" in Exercise 23.3.

2. Give referral sources here and have trainees to add to and possibly modify the list from Exercise 22.3.

3. Divide the training group into triads and appoint one a helper, one a helpee, and one an observer and ask them to discuss a personal example of a loss.

4. Have the observer give feedback and all play each role.

Homework for Trainees after Group Meeting

1. Have the trainees to write their concepts about their role as support to someone experiencing grief.

2. Prepare for Module 24 and Exercise 24.1.

MODULE **24**

ETHICAL CONSIDERATIONS IN PEER COUNSELING/PEER HELPING

Purposes

1. To enable trainees to learn some information concerning ethics.

2. To assist trainees in developing a local code of ethics and conduct.

3. To assist trainees in learning how to refer.

4. To assist trainees in establishing a network.

Approximate Time

Module 24—Introduction
Homework—10 minutes

Exercise 24.1—30 to 60 minutes

Exercise 24.2—60 to 120 minutes

Exercise 24.3—120 to 160 minutes

Exercise 24.4—60 minutes

Exercise 24.5—60 minutes
Homework—30 minutes

Exercise 24.6—60 minutes

Materials

Peer Power, Book 2, Applying Peer Helper Skills (workbook) one copy for each trainee

Code of Ethics, NPHA

Local referral sources

Introduction to Module

This module is probably one of the most important modules in the program. Therefore it might be good to do before you start training, at the start of the peer helping projects, and to review it regularly. The trainer should also write for the *Code of Ethics for the Facilitator and Program Standards* and *Peer Helper Code of Ethics* from the NPHA.

Training Procedures

1. Decide the number of training sessions and exercises to be included in this module.

2. Review the content to be covered in this module.

3. Be prepared with local resources, rules, laws, etc.

Evaluation Process

As a trainer, you can evaluate the process used in teaching this module by the finished Code of Ethics and Code of Conduct.

Measuring Outcomes

1. Use Exercise 24.5 to evaluate the learning.

2. As the peer helpers go through their various projects, observe how they are operating ethically, etc.

EXERCISE 24.1
ETHICAL ISSUES IN TRAINING

Purpose

To address some of the issues involved in training.

Introduction to Exercise

For the training to be fully effective, local norms must be addressed.

Training Procedures

1. Review the "Issues Important During Training" as listed in *Peer Power, Book 2, Applying Peer Helper Skills* (workbook). Add other points necessary to accommodate the local situation.

2. Discuss each one that fits your training program.

3. Ask the trainees to brainstorm the local norms and consequences for breaking them.

4. Write the finished product, duplicate it, and ask each trainee to sign it.

EXERCISE 24.2
CODE OF ETHICS FOR THE PEER COUNSELOR/HELPER

Purpose

To help the trainees learn about a national code of ethics and develop a local code of ethics.

Introduction to Exercise

In Exercise 24.2, the trainees will learn the national code of ethics and develop a local code of ethics.

Training Procedures

1. Review the national code of ethics.
2. Go over each major point listed in *Peer Power, Book 2, Applying Peer Helper Skills* (workbook).
3. Develop a local code of ethics and ask some of the peer counselors to finalize it.
4. Have the counselors sign a local code of ethics.

EXERCISE 24.3
KNOWING YOUR OWN LIMITS

Purposes

1. To know how to refer.
2. To understand the limits of peer helping.

Introduction to Exercise

A list of possible local referrals is very important for each peer helper. To assure a quality program for helpers a wise procedure is to have peer helpers talk to you before giving a referral to determine the appropriateness.

Training Procedures

1. Discuss the referral sources. You might have peer helpers call the local referral sources to get information.

2. Have the peer helpers write to national organizations to obtain a list of local providers.

3. Discuss the guidelines for referral.

4. Develop local guidelines for referral.

5. Have trainees sign an agreement for referral techniques.

EXERCISE 24.4
CODE OF CONDUCT

Purpose

To develop a code of conduct based on local regulations and laws.

Introduction to Exercise

Each local program must follow state laws and local regulations, plus program guidelines. Each peer counselor must also serve as a role model.

Training Procedures

1. Discuss trust (e.g., role model).

2. Discuss state laws (e.g., child abuse).

3. Discuss local regulations (e.g., drug free).

4. Discuss program norms (e.g., referral).

5. Discuss your own personal code of conduct (e.g., being loyal to peer helpee).

6. Have the helpers develop and approve their own code of conduct.

EXERCISE 24.5
DEALING WITH ETHICAL ISSUES

Purpose

To discuss actual situations and relate them to the code of ethics and code of conduct.

Introduction to Exercise

One way to teach ethics is the case-by-case approach.

Training Procedures

1. Review both the national and local code of ethics. Review the code of conduct.
2. Review the examples and refer to the problems with the codes.
3. Discuss the consequences for violations.
4. Have the peer helpers brainstorm additional situations.

Homework for Trainees after Group Meeting

Prepare for Exercise 24.6.

EXERCISE 24.6
NETWORKING

Purpose

To help the peer helpers set up a network.

Introduction to Exercise

Peer helpers need to understand networking and the need for networking. Then help them establish a local network as well as other ways to network.

Training Procedures

1. Discuss the concept of networking:

   a. The benefits.

   b. How it helps individuals.

2. Discuss local networking:

   a. How it is now.

   b. How to expand.

3. Discuss networking with others.

   a. Help them plan to meet with other peer helpers.

   b. Help them plan to write to other peer helpers.

   c. Hold a local conference.

   d. Other

4. Have the group develop a plan and assist them with their plan.

ADDITIONAL RESOURCES
by Judith A. Tindall, Ph.D.

(available from Accelerated Development Inc. Publishers, 3808 W. Kilgore Avenue, Muncie, Indiana 47304-4896, 1-800-222-1166)

Feelings: The 3 Rs—Receiving, Reflecting, Responding, by Judith A. Tindall, Ph.D., and Shirley Salmon, Ph.D.

Peer Programs: An In-depth Look at Peer Helping—Planning, Implementation, and Administration

Peer Power, Book 1, Workbook: Becoming an Effective Peer Helper and Conflict Mediator, Third Edition

Peer Power, Book 1, Strategies for the Professional Leader: Becoming an Effective Peer Helper and Conflict Mediator, Third Edition

Peer Power, Book 2: Applying Peer Helper Skills, Second Edition (workbook for trainee)

Peers Helping Peers: Program for the Preadolescent, Leader Manual, by Judith A. Tindall, Ph.D., and Shirley Salmon-White, Ph.D.

Peers Helping Peers: Program for the Preadolescent, Student Workbook, by Judith A. Tindall, Ph.D., and Shirley Salmon-White, Ph.D.

Audio Tape: ***Problem Solving***

JUDITH A. TINDALL, Ph.D.

LICENSED PSYCHOLOGIST,
L.P.C., N.B.C.C.

Dr. Tindall has been involved in training peer helpers and professionals in schools, community agencies, and churches since the late 60s. For the last several years, she has been in private practice as a psychologist and consultant with Rohen and Associates Psychological Center in St. Charles, Missouri. Prior to this, she worked for 18 years in public schools as a counselor, peer helping coordinator, and guidance director. She has been a consultant to and has conducted workshops with businesses, schools, governmental agencies, church groups, and hospitals concerning a wide range of topics.

Dr. Tindall has been in leadership positions in local, state, and national professional organizations. She was on the founding board and still serves on the National Peer Helping Association Board of Directors and is former chair of the Ethics and Standards Committee, co-chairs the Training and Consulting Committee, and serves on the Executive Committee as vice president. She was the start-up president of Missouri Peer Helpers Association.

She is author or co-author of several professional books (see previous page). She also has been guest editor twice for the Peer Facilitator Quarterly, and she has written numerous articles concerning peer helping, caring for yourself, group work, team building, leadership, eating disorders, wellness stress management, and type development.